FREUD: THE PARIS NOTEBOOKS

FREUD:
The Paris Notebooks

MATT COHEN

Quarry Press

"Freud, *il dottore*" and "Mostly Madame Larousse" were first published in French translation in the book *Freud à Paris*, XYZ Editeur, 1990.

The publisher thanks The Canada Council and the Ontario Arts Council for assistance in producing this book.

CANADIAN CATALOGUING IN PUBLICATION DATA

Cohen, Matt, 1942-
  Freud

ISBN 1-55082-004-4

  I. Title.

PS8555.O4F75 1991   C813'.54   C91-090148-1
PR9199.3.C64F73 1991

Cover art entitled *Nude on a Yellow Sofa* by Henri Matisse,
reproduced by permission of the National Gallery of Canada.
Design and imaging by ECW Type & Art, Oakville, Ontario.
Printed and bound by Hignell Printing, Winnipeg, Manitoba.

Published by *Quarry Press, Inc.*, P.O. Box 1061, Kingston, Ontario
K7L 4Y5 and P.O. Box 348, Clayton, New York 13408.

CONTENTS

FREUD, IL DOTTORE

1 A FEW THOUGHTS ON LOVE DISAPPOINTED

Robert Freud, *il dottore*, looked down from his third floor window to the teeming crowds on the Boulevard Raspail. Some were former patients, some were future patients, to some he was and always would be entirely unknown. Never mind, today he felt for each and every one of them a fierce and passionate love.

Freud, *il dottore*, stood at his window and blew a kiss at a particularly attractive creature wearing spiked heels and carrying an umbrella. "I love you," he hummed.

She turned around. Freud now noticed that there was a zipper dividing the left and right sides of her dress. At her throat was the zipper's ring, waiting to be pulled. Of course there was no way she could have heard him through the double glass of his office window. And even were the windows open his little song would have been drowned in the noise of the traffic.

Nonetheless, she turned around and retraced her steps. Below the office of the doctor was a branch of the Banque Nationale de Paris. No doubt such a woman had lots of money, multiple accounts hedged in a wide variety of currencies. What else could you do? Safety was these days no cigar. Even in Switzerland the banks were starting to show their books; the doctor could not help remembering the newspaper report of some former dictator whose Swiss accounts were being opened for inspection — opened and then emptied. Of course, it was wrong for a dictator to steal from the people. Even if he was stealing money that would have been wasted on some public monument. On the other hand, the Swiss banks were setting a bad example to their other customers. If a former dictator could not trust his bank, what hope was there for a poor shopkeeper or doctor who had spent his whole life trying to provide for his old age so he would not become a ward of the state?

The doctor turned from his window. Love and money did not mix; he had said it a thousand times.

Marry for money, he advised his female patients. Marry and stay married. Love and money may not mix, but money and sex — *there* is a combination you can count on. As for love — well — love had little to do with anything. Love wasn't something you felt for your husband or wife — even less your lover. Love was what you felt for children, or for the whole world on a sunny day, or — every year or ten — for a beautiful passing stranger.

"Let me tell you," he had told many, "there is nothing so insane as the idea of love. It is a myth we are enslaved to, the dangerous delusion of our time, a stupid romantic idea that no more belongs in the human mind than does a finger in the nose." The part about the finger in the nose always got a reaction but the doctor retained it in his rehearsed diatribe because he knew that — in the end, *enfin*, the only way to defeat myth was with metaphor. But he wasn't sure it really communicated the message. But then, what message? His patients did not want his messages, his cures, even his financial advice. Ultimately what they wanted was to be able to say to themselves and their friends that they were spending three hours a week in the office of the famous Robert Freud, *il dottore*, the Italian nephew of the immortal Sigmund.

Not that he followed his famous relation entirely.

The couch? Yes, he retained that; after all there is a dignity in tradition. But free association and the minute search for unconscious clues — what a joke. Sigmund, the German, had loved to exercise his genius by setting it to retrieve the obvious in the most laborious possible way. That was Germans for you. But he, Robert Freud, could read a patient's neurosis the way a pilot reads the topography of a country spread-eagled below him.

Freud looked at his watch: seventeen minutes after twelve. How perfect it would be to have a one o'clock appointment with the striking stranger he had seen through his window, to be meeting her at an excellent restaurant in Bologna where they would have a first course of grilled artichokes and chilled rosé. For the second course — why not Venice in a gondola, cheap and obvious but away from the crowds . . .

"Robert Freud?"

The stranger herself stood in the open doorway. She had pronounced his name in an unsatisfactory imitation of Italian, yet he did not know in which of his many languages to reply until she asked, in English, "Are you the doctor?"

"At your service."

"And you are truly the Italian relation of the famous Sigmund Freud?"

"I am," sighed the doctor.

"Well," said the woman, "I'm so glad to have found you." She put her hand to her throat and for a tantalizing moment Freud thought she was going to grasp the ring, pull down the long zipper of her dress, and reveal all to him. Why not? After all, he was the doctor and she the one wanting to confess. Soon he would know details more intimate than mere flesh.

"Sit," said the doctor. "During the first appointment there is no need to lie down. Are you in pain? Prepare to be soothed. Pain has no more place in the human heart than does a finger in the —"

"Unhh —" gasped the woman. From beneath her dress she extracted something. It flew across the room towards the doctor until, in his chest, there was a dark expanding pain. Across the woman's beautiful features raged a battle between triumph and neurosis. The doctor fell to his knees. He saw the woman's open mouth, a black emptiness. "Oh, my God," the woman said. As the doctor's body began to flatten into the rug he jerked a hand up to where he had been hit, plunged his palm into the now spreading blood which was gradually soaking through his shirt.

The woman knelt beside him. "It's so beautiful," she crooned.

She was leaning over him, her body gradually lowering itself towards his, and the doctor finally realized what was happening. This woman, a rape-terrorist, had a hitherto unrecorded pathology which made it impossible for her to reach satisfaction except through sexual intercourse with a dying man. Then he had a second insight, a more explosive and universal one — he realized that *all* women were subject to this weird prenecrophilia, that the great driving unconscious force of the whole female sex was to enjoy the last moment of their partner's life. Soon she would be kneeling beside him, soon she would be greedily kissing him, soon she would be tearing off her clothes and pressing her unzipped self against him, soon she would be moaning: "Doctor, doctor, I've been wanting this for months. I came here to be cured but then — when I saw you — doctor, I can't explain it, everything started to buzz and whir. Doctor, can you help me?"

The doctor withdrew his hand from his shirt. Red, yes, it was covered with red. But he wasn't dying. A bag of gummy red fluid had exploded against the knot in his tie and was now dripping through his clothes and running down his skin.

"Do you mind if I take your picture?"

Flash. Flash. The woman was prancing about him like an over-excited nanny goat. With every burst of the flashbulb he could see his image in the cheap magazines.

Robert Freud struggled to sit up. He stroked his triangular beard. Then, without further hesitation, he spoke in his most reassuring voice. "Lie down," he commanded. "Rest your weary head and close your eyes. Are you in pain? Prepare to be soothed. Pain has no more place —"

2 A LITTLE NIGHT
MUSIC: PART I

That evening Freud stood at the bathroom mirror. On the counter in front of him were protractors, tape measures, compasses, a pair of nail scissors, horizontal and vertical levels. It wasn't easy, cutting his beard in a triangle, making the two long sides appear exactly the same length. Nor did the point of his beard line up with the center of his face merely by wishing it so. He had often said as much to his wife. Forces were at work: the natural disequilibrium of the human brain, a childhood accident to one cheek, the inevitable propensity of beard hair to warp slightly under humid conditions.

"Robert, we are already late."

"Yes my love." Freud gave a last snip to an errant

hair. No one knew his secret: during the summer, when the weather was damp, he raised the point of his beard one half centimeter towards his chin. Also, he didn't really cut the sides the same length — one was shorter to compensate for the cheek muscles that had atrophied after his sister had shot him in a fit of jealous rage.

"Robert, the Opera will start without us." Over the years Eleanour's voice had gradually dried out, as though over-use had transformed once supple vocal cords into leather thongs. "Robert, do you hear me?"

"Yes," Freud said, "I was just listening to you." He rubbed his chest — the place where the blood had exploded. When he had come home, shirt stained, he had wondered how Eleanour would react.

"What a mess!" she had cried as he came through the door. "How many times have I told you not to eat spaghetti for lunch?"

Now she was talking about the opera again. "Which one are we going to tonight?"

"It's not an opera," Freud said. "it's an opening. One of my patients is an artist."

"What kind of artist? These days anyone without a job is an artist. Did I tell you about Maria's son?"

"Yes," said Freud, although in fact he couldn't

recall the story. Anyway it would end the way all his wife's stories ended, which was with a few muttered words and the sucking of lips. For a moment he felt guilty for thinking his wife unattractive. But she was happily chattering away about something else and — anyway — he remembered that just the other day he had admired the skin of her shoulders or some such thing. And so his attention returned to the knotting of his tie, a special silk number his own analyst had given him as a graduation present — one to be worn only on days when he had commenced relations with a new patient.

3 THE AFTERNOON IN THE GARDEN

The afternoon is stifling. Overhead the sun pulses behind an oppressive milky mist.

The boy standing under the beech tree is too young to make conversation about the weather. He knows only that a long-awaited day has arrived, and that he is not enjoying it. Because the occasion is formal he is dressed in thick British tweeds which have made his skin break into a rash. "My God," his mother exclaimed when he emerged, "in those you look like a real English boy." In fact, he has a passport to prove it, though like his father he was born in Italy. Now he wishes they were back home, instead of in this foreign country which is supposed to be his own.

Sitting near the boy, under the shade of the same tree, the old man looks out across the lawn. He too is in exile, though in his case the exile is more complete. That is to say, the old man has left not only the country of his youth, the language of his youth, to say nothing of youth itself — but somehow he has made another voyage. That was the voyage he had always feared: the voyage from clarity to dimness, from dimness to not caring. The mind which had spent a lifetime leaping acrobatically from one clue to another now wanted little more than pure sensation. Opening his eyes he could let the colors of the afternoon soak through his brain. By turning his head he could see a shifting panorama of leaves, manicured grass, striped lawnchairs set out for the daily influx of visitors.

"Dr. Freud, what an honor . . ." "Dr. Freud we are so glad you consented to come . . ." "Doctor, Doctor, Doctor . . ." When he was young, studying medicine in Paris and Vienna, that was when he might have become a real doctor. That was when you could make a game of counting the rats you saw while making the rounds, when doctors carried their sutures in their pockets, when blood-stained clothes weren't changed from one week to the next. The stench, the hopelessness of being sick. The long days spent on the wards, the evenings in the laboratories, the midnight letter to Martha. "My dearest, my dearest . . ." Sweet cocaine roaring through his brain. White lightning.

"Dr. Freud, Dr. Freud . . ." The boy shaped his mouth carefully around the words. "Dr. Freud?"

"Yes?" The boy looked at the old man's face. He had heard about the operations on the jaw, the prothesis inside the mouth. "You see," his mother had said, "that's what comes from smoking." And then, before the great day, she had of course warned him not to stare.

But the old man was staring at him and the boy couldn't help returning it. The beard partially hid the mottled skin, the jaw was twisted out of shape, even through the thick lenses the skin beneath the old man's eyes formed dark sinister bruises.

"I came to say hello," the boy said.

"Good."

"This is the first time," said the boy.

"What's your name?"

"Robert Freud." He said the second name quickly as he always did.

"Good," said the old man. When he spoke, the boy noticed, his lips moved but his teeth stayed fixed, as though he were a talking doll. Then the lips stopped moving and the face slumped slightly forward so that the old man's chin was almost resting on his chest.

The boy became aware of the heat again. His collar was chafing. He shrugged his shoulder to make his shirt scratch itself against his neck. Then he shifted his feet.

"Well," said the old man.

"Well," said the boy. He prepared to leave. "Thank you for talking to me."

"I could tell you a story," said the old man. "Did you ever hear the one about the giant green frog?"

"No."

"It's a good one," said the old man. He saw the boy moving towards him. The sun's embrace grew warmer. He closed his eyes, trying to remember what he had just said. He slipped into sleep.

4 SUCKED DRY BY VAMPIRES

In Trevanien's glass a certain amount of wine remained, making a dark red surface that challenged Trevanien to add to it, to drink from it, to lose himself in another wasted day.

"The point is," said Trevanien, "people are coming to the conclusion that he was a fraud. I even read a claim somewhere that he didn't cure a single patient."

"The psyche is not a wound which heals over."

"The point is," Trevanien began again. And then he stopped. The point was, Trevanien had been about to say, that the American public *cared* about Sigmund Freud; for them he was on a par with

Abraham Lincoln and Albert Einstein as a founding father of the twentieth century. Trevanien looked across the table at Robert Freud. This man, the nephew or the eighth cousin or whatever he was, must surely find it strange living in such a famous shadow. At the same time, there was something very out of season about Robert Freud. Middle-aged, vaguely decayed, he had the slightly battered look of all European intellectuals. Despite their casually impressive learning, their multiple languages, the sophisticated political stances that took more twists than a snake in heat, they were all refugees from some previous era — probably one that had never existed.

"Have some more wine, we can't waste it."

"Thank you." Trevanien watched as the level climbed towards the lip of his glass.

"You spent some time in England, didn't you? Your English is really excellent."

"Thank you. We came to London just before the war, and I stayed on until I was ready to go to medical school."

"And why did you choose Paris? Didn't your family come from Italy?"

"My father."

"And Paris?"

"I don't know. I suppose Paris has always seemed

a congenial place to be in exile. You must know something about that."

"I'm only a journalist. For me, exile is just an extension of the umbilical cord." Trevanien, hearing his own words, wondered what they were supposed to mean. "In any case," Trevanien continued, "the reason I wanted to interview you is this whole cocaine affair. Not that it's really something new — everyone has known for decades that your uncle published papers on cocaine and even used it himself. But now that the new correspondence has been released people are saying that he was a cocaine addict and all his theories can be explained away as part of his addiction."

"As you yourself point out, it's nothing new."

"But the publicity is new. And so, therefore's the damage it could do his reputation." Trevanien sipped at his wine. Only a few hours ago, this meeting had seemed an inspired idea. Robert Freud, after all, was not totally unknown. And with his narrow face, pointed beard and wideset eyes, he looked enough like his uncle that photographs of the two men, side by side, would assure the article's success. Trevanien had even found, in an old magazine, a photograph of the young Robert Freud visiting the old man in London. That was after Freud had fled the Germans in Vienna. He had probably already been senile; nonetheless, Trevanien was counting on Freud to give him some sort of anecdote about the old man's hard-earned wisdom.

"Mr. Trevanien, I'd like to help you. I do care about my uncle's reputation, although as you know I do not practice psychoanalysis in the way he did. But surely all this fuss about his use of cocaine will pass. It was an experiment. Does that discredit his theories? Drugs have been a staple part of almost every culture that has ever existed. Whether they improve, destroy, have any effect at all is surely unknown. Perhaps their existence through history merely shows that the genetic structure of the species has provided us with a biological door that opens us to addiction. Perhaps drugs are man's way of altering his mind to make a bridge with the infinite."

"Can I quote you on that?"

"Freud's nephew advocates use of illegal drugs? That would be an excellent headline, Mr. Trevanien. But your articles are surely too — tasteful — for that."

"Correct, Dr. Freud. Even we journalists have our scruples." Trevanien beckoned to the waiter. "All this talk about drugs is making me thirsty. And I happen to have with me some very excellent Cuban cigars. Will you join me Dr. Freud?" Trevanien withdrew the packet of cigars from his breast pocket and opened it up, extending it across the table. The aroma of tobacco burst out of the metal box. Trevanien watched Freud's face as he hesitated. His own lower lip began to tremble. This whole situation was ridiculous. Here he was again, playing the role he had promised to give up, the role of the young man who wanted to charm, who would *kill* himself to charm. And yet he couldn't help it: he wanted Robert Freud to accept the cigar and prolong the meal, he *needed* Freud to give himself up to this meeting, this conversation, this stupid idea that his uncle's reputation — the whole future of the human mind — lay waiting to be decided by Trevanien's typewriter. His lip was trembling, he could feel his heart pounding; his body had gone rigid in an effort to keep his hand from shaking; and yet, even while his nervous system was going out of control he struggled to keep the casual smile in place.

"Thank you," Robert Freud said. He reached for the cigar.

"My pleasure." The cigars were lit, the cognac was being poured. Doctor, Trevanien imagined himself saying, do you know that I have a vested interest in this whole story? Do you know that I've had two nervous breakdowns and underwent shock treatments both times? Do you know that I don't care about sex anymore, except when I'm stoned? With cocaine, preferably, though in fact, if it's really good, I'd rather be alone. No insult intended, doctor, and anyway I don't really want to be cured. I just thought I'd drop by to talk about it. Not the sex, I mean, or the drugs, but the drinking. Or maybe all of them together. I never minded the idea of being an alcoholic but I think it's starting to drag me down. Even the wet blanket effect is something I can cope with, doctor, but I think it might be eating me out from inside. Doctor, please help me, I'm being sucked dry by vampires.

5 A LITTLE NIGHT MUSIC: PART II

Night. A cool summer sky. Leather soles making melodies of meditation along the sidewalk. Freud, *il dottore*, who lives not so far from métro Emile Zola, is pacing the streets of his district. His hands are jammed in his pockets. He walks by a newspaper store where the owner has crippled fingers. He walks by a store he has never visited, a shop that specializes in mildly erotic lingerie. The doctor is thinking. He turns down a street called Rue du Théâtre. He thinks about the fact that on this street nothing has ever happened to him. Nor will it now. The night is late. Few other people are out. The doctor's footsteps echo against the high walls which frame the narrow street. The doctor is thinking.

The doctor is not thinking. The doctor is drifting in a paper gondola along the short length of canal remaining before he is irrevocably dumped into the polluted sea of old age. The doctor is in the prime of life. The doctor never had a life. The doctor is thinking about his childhood in a small Italian town, the way his father wasted his life selling grilled artichokes in front of monuments so that his children could go to good schools. The doctor is thinking about his childhood in London and wondering if people suspect he acquired his Italian accent by watching Sophia Loren movies. The doctor spits his Mexican cigar into a gutter. He goes into an apartment building. It is post war, which means it has a marble facade, an elevator with folding doors, central heating that almost always works. Set into the marble-faced inside wall is a mirror. He looks and sees that he resembles himself. He takes the elevator with folding doors six floors up, turns to the right, unlocks the door of his apartment. When he gets into bed his wife is asleep. She is breathing slow heavy breaths. Beneath the sheet is a planet of warmth and cologne, mountains of muscles eroding into fat, valleys of thickened skin and adipose tissue. The doctor lies on his back and clasps his hands across his belly. He closes his eyes. He drifts. He sleeps.

He sleeps. He dreams. He is in an imaginary boat drifting along rivers of pure memory. The boat dissolves. He is swimming in a thick current of imprinted neurons, a jumbled alphabet soup of possibilities flow by him. Long tangled strings of synapses cling to his fingers and toes. "Why am I struggling?" he asks himself. To dream, to drown. To lie buried in the primal mud until finally the heart stops beating. Then death. The oppressive river lightens, turns clear and lucent, scatters itself into ten billion stars flung across the sky. To die, to be released.

6 MEASURES TO BE TAKEN IN THE ABSENCE OF WHITE LIGHTNING

From his office Trevanien telephoned his wife. There was no answer, which meant she had already left for the party. After putting a message on his machine, Trevanien ran down the stairs into the lobby.

An American journalist in Paris, Trevanien was, according to the man from the State Department, a prime target for kidnapping. "Just the kind that can give them publicity."

Before crossing the street he was to look both ways for guerillas; before getting into his car he was to check for them in the back seat. Also to look beneath for a bomb-like object wired to go off when he started the motor. Suspicious packages were to be taken to the Embassy, wrong numbers or obscene phone calls noted, strange noises outside the apartment or in the street below treated as warnings of impending disaster.

Trevanien got into his car. He felt in an undesirable limbo, a swaying bridge between the mellow taste of good cognac gone slightly bilious and the definitively queasy sensations he would experience if he woke up drunk in the middle of the night. He reached for his glove compartment, then — as the man from the state department had advised him — looked under it. No suspicious wires or molotov cocktails. He opened the compartment. "I don't need to tell you this," the man had added, "but you should never accept drugs from strangers." The pills Trevanien now swallowed had come not from a stranger, but from his doctor, an understanding expatriate Swede for whom Trevanien had once helped to arrange a passport. The problem was, the doctor had explained to him one night when Trevanien arrived in particularly deplorable condition, the problem was all in the blood — the blood that was addicted, the blood that sought what it needed even though it was poisoned by its own needs.

Trevanien, sweating and shaking, had rolled up

his shirtsleeve so that the doctor could give him an injection. When the needle was withdrawn a few drops of his unfortunately victimized blood made a trail down the inside of his forearm.

"At least you don't use needles," the doctor said. "If you ever start doing that, I won't be able to help you." And so, despite his new vision of his blood as a polluted lagoon, Trevanien was able to leave the doctor's office reassured that his problem, no matter how unpleasant at times, whatever it was, was not like those problems you read about in the papers, the problems of rock stars or junkies risking death to feed their habit. The fact was, as he had told his wife, he was just a typical member of the middle class — a weak-willed focus of more tension than his nervous system was designed to accommodate.

When the pills were down Trevanien looked in the rearview mirror. No one was following him. On the other hand it is not so easy to follow a parked car. Trevanien turned on the ignition. The gas exploded in the cylinders, but only in the sequence and manner intended by the manufacturer.

As he swung around the Place Charles Michel Trevanien put a cassette into his tape deck. When the music was adjusted to his satisfaction he began winding his way towards the party where he was

34

supposed to meet his wife. Soon he was illegally parked in a narrow alleyway filled with cars more expensive than his own. At a set of iron-grilled doors he punched in the code that released the electronic lock and let him into a large and elegant garden. From the open window of one of the surrounding apartments came the sounds of a party nearing its height. Trevanien went in the open doorway, paused at the marble foyer to admire the renaissance sculptures with which Madame Roissy liked to decorate her entranceway, then climbed the oblig- atory spiral staircase until he came to the apartment itself.

Professor Roissy, or more correctly now, Second Consul Roissy, had been on leave from his post in the Department of Art History at the University of Gotteborg when Trevanien first met him at a reception at the American Embassy. Now he was a rapidly rising star in the Swedish diplomatic service. He was also at the desirable end of a family fortune which he had twice subjected to major escalations: once by buying into British oil companies just before the OPEC cartel jacked up the price in the early seventies; then a second time by selling short just before the cartel collapsed. "For an intellectual you spend a lot of time making money," Trevanien had once said to him.

"I am only moving with the times," Roissy had replied. "Sweden has already had her share of starving artists."

Suave, well-dressed, confident, Roissy was the type who would have sailed through the American private schools Trevanien had attended. But Roissy, unlike Trevanien, had learned his languages and his art appreciation the old-fashioned moneyed way — by going to expensive European boarding schools and then spending summers with relatives in the various capitals.

Within Roissy's apartment the noise of the party had peaked at a deafening roar. Trevanien snatched a drink from a passing tray, then, turning to orient himself, found himself pushed into the back of a former mistress, a one-time stringer for *The New York Times* who was now married to a Belgian bank officer. For the second time that day Trevanien found himself thinking about his sex life. Somehow he had passed from plotting future liaisons to sinking into old ones. Helen Spender was her name. She was tanned, suitably jewelled, expensively dressed. "We should get together sometime," she was saying. Because of the noise Trevanien wasn't sure exactly what she was suggesting. He tried to remember the texture of their last encounter, the sexual details, but could only picture the hotel room, the rumpled bed with the pillows pushed onto the floor, his own desire to be downstairs in the bar, having a drink and sincerely wishing her the best in her married life to come. "We must," Helen said. Trevanien worked on recalling the exact sensations of being inside her. Warm, cold, slippery, dry — it all escaped him. Perhaps, he wondered, he would only remember these details when he was dying. But he was happy to be with her now, to be pressed against her, to know that there was an oasis of acceptance in an otherwise jangled situation. "But I'm only thirty-seven years old," Trevanien found himself saying. "Thirty-seven!" Helen Spender exclaimed. "I always thought you were younger. Imagine that, you must have lied to me about your age. Come on, tell me the truth." She put her hand on Trevanien's shirt.

"Vous désirez, monsieur?" A voluptuous nymph exposed her decolletage while leaning forward to offer a canapé which time and heat had transformed from succulent salmon mousse into a miniature pinkish lesson in erosion and dehydration. Trevanien imagined himself writing the lead to a story on diplomatic parties . . . "On the embassy circuit in Paris each country displays its wealth and its power not by the presence of military force, but by the amount and quality of naked skin offered to the

visitor." Of course this wasn't precisely true, but neither was anything else that the American press printed about events outside its borders. And anyway, if it wasn't true it was at least amusing. And if it wasn't amusing, it was at least what was expected of George Hinton Trevanien, only child of parents who may or may not have been ruined in the Great Crash, private school boy, one-time President of the Harvard Debating Club who had sealed his financial future in that most-respected of Harvard traditions — by marrying into one of Boston's great fortunes.

"Cigarette?"

"I quit," Trevanien said.

"Everyone's stopping these days. You'd think they were going to live forever."

"This was a New Year's promise to Sandy. Anyway, I cheat, I smoke cigars."

"Is she here?"

"In the corner, talking to her friends from the Ministry." The French Ministry of Culture, he meant, because in fact this party was supposed to be one of the great cultural events of the season: a member of the Swedish Academy had come to Paris to interview French writers and this was taken as a sign that another Nobel Prize in Literature was on its way. In a month or so this would provide an excellent article — the speculation about whether the French winner would be a popular writer or one of those arcane literary experimentalists the Academy loved to pluck from oblivion.

"And are you still the perfect couple?"

Trevanien looked down at Helen. Her eyes were wideset, blue; above them arched wispy blonde eyebrows with fine tiny hairs that used to curl when she perspired. Her hair, too, was blonde. During their affair — if that's what it had been — or maybe they had only been sleeping together — her hair had been long and bleached almost white by the sun. "My college girl look," she had said then. "If you ever see me with a proper haircut you'll know I've finally started to grow up." Now her hair was a darker honey color and it *was* cut properly — into one of those shapes that Trevanien recognized as being popular that winter in Paris.

"Look, I've got to go. Give me a call next week and we'll fix something up." She kissed him quickly, four little French pecks, and then suddenly Trevanien was standing alone, surrounded by the backs of busily chattering strangers.

He looked down at his hands. He was holding a cigarette that he didn't remember lighting. Another stranger in a low dress came by with drinks. Trevanien helped himself, this time feeling a sudden and ridiculous desire to bend over and kiss the exposed mounds of breast. Sex, he thought to himself, for a man who has supposedly rejected it I seem to think of nothing else. The cigarette was half-gone but he couldn't remember smoking any of it. His glass was still full. He edged his way over to a table, stubbed out the cigarette and put down his glass. Looking up he saw one of the French writers who would be hoping to be interviewed by the Swedish Academician.

"Suzanne," he said, as she knifed towards him.

"Trevanien, *ça va?*"

Thin, with long dark hair, Suzanne fell into what Trevanien called the "tortured intellectual" category. The flesh beneath her eyes was dark and bruised, her fingers were stained and burned by innumerable filterless cigarettes, her smile was quick but sad. "We're going to the restaurant afterwards with you and your wife. Stephan is coming too. Have you met him yet?"

"Stephan?"

"The man from the Academy. Now don't look so unhappy. Do you want me to get you a drink?"

7 RICHARD AND ELIZABETH OR THROWING BLOOD

"When did you first know you were an artist?" Freud, *il dottore*, leaned back in his recliner.

He watched Judith's face. A disappointed look passed over it before she replied, "It came to me in the night."

In his hands Freud was holding a review he had clipped from the morning paper. A review of the opening he had attended with his wife the night before. "Richard and Elizabeth is your first exhibition of sculptures. But it was very successful in North America before it was brought here. You must be very pleased."

"When I was a little girl I wanted to be Elizabeth Taylor but then I discovered Richard Burton."

"And then you wanted to be him?"

"No, I mean I found out that he destroyed her."

"In your sculptures it seems the figures are not simply making love but are also struggling for supremacy. Is this your view of Richard and Elizabeth or of sexual relations in general?"

"Boy, they don't call you Freud for nothing." Nervous laugh. "That was the idea — that they would be making love, I mean. But then they began acting — as it were — on their own. After that came the chains and knives, etc. Also the blood.

"That's why I'm here, Doctor Freud. You see, doctor, I have a strange compulsion to throw blood. The first time was when I was in the bus station in Thunder Bay, on the way to Saskatoon to visit my parents for Christmas. The next time was at my boyfriend's 25th birthday party. On the way to the party I bought a bag of chicken livers, saying to myself they were a special treat for the cat. When I arrived, I slipped the livers out of the bag and then thinned the blood with ketchup and water. At the crucial moment — splat — I threw the bag against the wall. My boyfriend was very upset. I began reading books in order to cure myself, but none of them mentioned this disease. Meanwhile the compulsion was growing. I began to drop into butcher shops almost every day, buying sweetbreads or organ meats — then late at night I would go out and throw them at street signs or billboards. After all my reading, I was sure my pathology must be a revolt against authority. I went to see a therapist. After two months he gave up and said I needed full analysis. That was in Toronto. He said, however, that the only person he could recommend was you. He gave me your address. But I decided I couldn't afford to come to Paris. Then, one night at a feminist dinner party at 21 McGill I threw blood at the headwaiter. They threatened to call the police until I explained I had committed not a crime but an act of cultural sabotage. On the spot, everyone dug into their purses and raised the fare for me to come here. One of the women even had a sister with a restaurant where I work as a waitress. When I got here, I delayed coming to see you. For a while it seemed as though I might have undergone some sort of miraculous spontaneous cure. Then, a few days ago, I found myself buying sheep's entrails at a butcher's store. I realized you were the next target."

"And last night?"

"That, doctor, was art. Or so I told myself in my sickness. My first intention was to cut myself and splash the blood on Richard and Elizabeth. But to tell the truth I'm a bit squeamish. Then I thought of ketchup or paint. But that's so cheap, it gives art a bad name. So it was back to animal blood. An hour after the door opened, it would be announced I was going to read a group of poems dedicated to Richard and Elizabeth. Mixed media is very big in Canada, doctor. As I read the poems, I would go from figure to figure, splashing them with blood. At the beginning everything went as planned. But there were so many people, the reaction was so strong, and when I turned to look at you, doctor, you seemed so full of sympathy for me. I admit I lost control. And I'm so terribly sorry about your wife —"

8 LIVING ON WATER

It was raining steadily, a cold hard rain that had begun falling while they were still at the restaurant and now, if anything, was falling even more intensely. Until a few moments ago the sky had been utterly black. Trevanien was certain of this because for what seemed a very long time, though in fact possibly only a few minutes, he had been standing outside his office and staring up into the sky so that the rain could expend its full force on his face, sluice out the fatigue, the remnants of the drinks and the pills.

Trevanien was staring into the sky, and where there had been only blackness he now saw something else. Not exactly hope but at least a yellow-gray light along the eastern horizon. In a little while the yellow-gray stripe would become a window into the dawn. In a little while the rain would be eaten up by the yellow-gray dawn and the sky would take on the sheen of a newly-swallowed pearl. In that light, which Trevanien was convinced would soon arrive, the cafés would begin to open and he would find steaming hot coffee with a croissant and a glass of cognac to get him going. Because now, stone sober, he had nothing to fear from drink. Drink would not harm his blood or fog his brain when he was in this condition; in this condition he was the master of his own blood, his own body, his own consciousness.

Trevanien was standing outside his office. Before that he had been inside his office, and before that he had been in a restaurant. But when it was time to go home he had told his wife he needed to work and then he had driven from the restaurant to the office where for a while he had lain on the couch with his eyes closed listening to the sound of the rain sliding down the window. Then without having even thought about it, he had gone to the telephone and dialled the number of Helen Spender. As her phone began to ring he remembered she had said that her husband was away. Which was fortunate, because the last thing Trevanien wanted was to get Helen into trouble with her husband. When she answered, he felt an amazing wave of relief.

"It's George, I didn't mean to wake you up."

"Christ, George, what are you doing? Is anything wrong?"

"No, I just needed to talk to you?"

"Let me get a cigarette."

Again Trevanien found himself sighing with relief, and while Helen got her cigarette he unwrapped one of the Cuban cigars he had offered Robert Freud. In the old days he had sometimes phoned like this, in the middle of the night. That was after his wife had rejoined him in Paris and he had tried to stop seeing Helen.

"Okay, here I am. Now, you better talk. What happened? Did your doctor tell you you were an alcoholic? Did Sandy finally kick you out? Did you go to bed with someone but couldn't get it up?"

"None of the above."

"Well?"

"I needed to talk to you, that's all. I was feeling lonely."

"You were feeling lonely." Helen's voice was sharp, sarcastic. Trevanien hung up. A few minutes later she called back and asked Trevanien if he wanted to come to see her.

"I think so," Trevanien said.

Now Trevanien was standing outside of his office,

watching the rain come down into his open eyes. He hadn't gone to see Helen, or perhaps he was still on his way to see Helen. In a few minutes he would get into his car and drive around until he found an open café. Helen would understand, perhaps Helen would even be grateful. Sandy would certainly be grateful, even though she had never found out about Helen and therefore didn't realize what she had to be grateful for, and then — finally but most importantly — he himself would be grateful because in the end Helen wasn't the answer, or even the question. In the end, Helen was a married woman and he was a married man, and you didn't endanger carefully made arrangements. Or at least you tried not to.

Trevanien stepped back into the shelter of his doorway. A car passed, yellow foglights sweeping the street like cat's eyes. He had written a story about headlights in Paris but never about the rain. The truth was that most Americans had no idea that Paris was subject to interminable rains. The American public thought of Paris as a sunny place full of cafés and jolly blue-overalled Frenchmen drinking two litres of red wine a day. They thought of the eternal sunshine on the cobbled streets of Montmartre and pictured the bright sunny posters that decorated their rooms. When they came to

Paris and found it full of beggars and purse-snatchers they complained to the American Embassy. The Embassy could give them advice on how to protect their money, but they couldn't do anything about the weather except advise them to try the Riviera.

"Try the Riviera," Trevanien said to himself. "Or try going home to your wife and having a good hot bath." Another car passed, another pair of cat's eyes. For a moment Trevanien wondered if it might be Helen, come to see if he had committed suicide. But it wasn't anybody, at least not anyone Trevanien knew, just a middle-aged man a few years older than himself who peered curiously at Trevanien and then after slowing down, continued on his way.

Trevanien walked down the street and got into his car. As he sat down he realized that he was soaked through. He began driving home, but then when he got to his apartment block he changed his mind and kept on driving. A few minutes later he saw a café with its doors open. He got out and had a coffee and a cognac. One to settle his stomach, one to dry him out. Then he got back into his car and let it drive itself to Helen's. If the lights were on he would go in. If they were off he would go home. It was as simple as that. "Right?" he asked aloud. "Right." When he arrived the lights were on.

9 THE PEACE THAT PASSETH UNDERSTANDING

Robert Freud, *il dottore*, was alone in his office. It was the beginning of March, a dark evening, and the steady rain which had begun in the morning was now giving way to a light drizzle. Freud turned out the lights of his office, poured himself a whiskey. When he had started his practice he had always had a drink like this, early in the winter evenings when he could sit in his darkened office and spend half an hour looking out at the street unobserved while the appointments which had filled his day unwound and his mind unknotted itself from the strain of following so many intricate stories.

In those days he had loved to relax, in those days his mind had contained a mode of relaxation, in those days it seemed there was still a mental "state of nature," a pure consciousness into which he could immerse himself at the end of the working day, or when he hiked through the mountains, or even in the middle of the night when he woke up consumed with worries about his patients or his daughter.

Now the walls between the compartments had become membranes easily penetrated. No matter how tortuous the path, it was like other paths he had followed. But at the end of the path lay not an oasis of contentment but merely fatigue. To sleep, to dream. To die, to be released.

To sleep, to dream. To live another life. Too late for that. Already fifty-six, nearing the end of middle age. As a child he had told himself middle age began at twenty-five and lasted until forty. After which old age. After which a state for which there were no words. Now he was fifty-six. There had been illnesses: two bouts with pneumonia — one leaving him gasping beneath an oxygen tent so that for two weeks he died the slow death of a landed fish. That, according to the doctor, had taken something from him which would not be replaced. Then there had been the removal of a lump from his left calf — after nights without sleep it had turned out to be benign. Followed by the cancer itself — skin cancer on one side of his forehead and along the ridges of his shoulder blades where his skin had crisped red every summer and peeled off in thin papery strips.

To die, to sleep. Fifty-six years old. There had been the various illnesses that might have been fatal — those were escapes; and on the other hand there were the various conditions that dragged at him: the chronically painful left kidney, the arthritis that periodically attacked his knee and hip, the high blood pressure that made the doctor talk about diets and stopping drinking. In sum, at fifty-six, he was not exactly bathing in the fountain of youth. On the other hand he had proved to be hardy, to be lucky, to be mildly cooperative when it came to preserving a minimum standard of health. Conclusion: twenty more years, possibly thirty.

Twenty more years, possibly thirty? What an incredible prospect!

Ten thousand days.

A quarter of a million hours.

Time enough to live new lives, travel new worlds, suffer new pains.

Freud set down his glass and pushed the recliner mechanism of his chair so that he was lying almost horizontal. This was his own couch. His listener was the dark evening air — always sympathetic, always discreet. To it he could confide his fear that he would never again leap from a rock into the ocean, never again exhaust himself having intercourse with a stranger, never again feel in the morning that life lay ahead of him — unlived, unspoiled, unknown.

And yet: ten thousand days, a quarter of a million hours. Time to build a boat, stick by stick, put it together, set off to sea in the hope of discovering new continents. Time to be inflamed by an idea, to stay up hundreds of nights making love to it, time to set it down in prose that would change the directions of men's minds. How had it happened? He had grown old but not dead. Exhausted but not content.

He closed his eyes. A peaceful feeling had begun to invade his blood. He wriggled to make himself comfortable in his chair. He was imagining himself going home, calmly telling Eleanour that he was leaving forever.

"How could you," she sobs, "after everything we've shared."

She screams, she shrieks, she rents her hair and knots the tassels of her dressing gown.

Freud, warmly ensconced in a bubble bath off the master bedroom, smokes a cigar and sips champagne.

"Don't you care? Don't you care? Don't you care?"

"Of course I care. But you see . . ." Here Freud pauses, blows a long stream of cigar smoke through the steamy air. "I have wider responsibilities."

"Then it's true," Eleanour shrieks. They both

53

know whereof she speaks. In a studio apartment near the Bastille, playing jazz records and inoculating herself with aphrodisiacs, lives a crazed sex goddess, an ex-student of Freud's who is utterly dependent on weekly all-night visits from the master to keep her from a terrible fate. "You promised me it would only be once a week," Eleanour screams. "I knew you'd run away with her. Admit the truth, you sanctimonious asshole."

At this moment Eleanour is standing above him. Static electricity has turned her normally limp dyed hair into red porcupine quills swollen with anger.

"No," Freud says, "there is someone else."

He has in mind a woman of infinite compassion, genius, and the beauty of true maturity. A woman whose voice is a rich golden contralto. A woman whose radiant soul melts all around her. A woman whose desire is to embrace Robert Freud, to restore him to the living, to endow each of his quarter of a million remaining hours with total perfection.

Freud gets out of the bath, in the same motion sweeping Eleanour into the sudsy water. Downstairs a limousine is waiting. As he dries himself he notices that for his former pudgy self has been substituted the body of Apollo.

"Eleanour." The bubbles part. She rises like Venus from the fronds.

10 EVERYTHING IS THROWN INTO INTO DOUBT — OUR HERO AND HIS FRIEND ARE FORCED TO MAKE PAINFUL DECISIONS — HOURS OF DARK- NESS BECOME CONFUSED WITH HOURS OF LIGHT — BATHTUBS RETAIN UTMOST IMPORTANCE

Trevanien stood at the doctor's desk, hands clasped behind his back as though he were his delinquent younger self summoned to the office of the head-master. Robert Freud was reading aloud from a newspaper clipping. "At a time when America is preparing itself for an all-out war against cocaine, a war whose first battles were unleashed by Sigmund Freud himself, Robert Freud remains calm, almost oblivious. At a luncheon the other day he declared that public reputations have no importance and that his only concern was for his patients. Meanwhile, like thousands of other analysts and psychiatrists, Robert Freud continues to practice a brand of medicine now known to have been dreamed up, as it were, in a series of drug-induced reveries. Despite the reluctance of Doctor Freud and other psychiatrists to comment to the press, the legitimacy of Sigmund Freud's theories is expected to be a topic of great controversy at a forthcoming meeting of . . ."

Robert Freud got up from his desk and walked over to the window. In that intense white light, Freud's face looked suddenly insubstantial and papery. "Why do you write this garbage?"

"It's my vocation to write garbage."

"I opened this office twenty years ago. At that time I was still finishing my thesis. You know what my adviser told me? 'Forget the theories when someone walks in the door. Those for whom you can have real feelings, they are the ones who should be your patients.' "

Trevanien joined Freud at the window. They were looking down at the teeming noon-time crowds on the Boulevard Raspail. Weaving her way through the crowds, half-walking, half-running, was an extraordinary woman. Despite the bright sun she was wearing a raincoat and carrying an umbrella. Directly beneath them she stopped and looked up. Trevanien now noticed that her raincoat was divided by a zipper with a large gold ring. It was pulled up to her neck, as though beneath it she were naked. She began walking again. Trevanien looked at Freud. He too was following her progress.

Trevanien pulled out a package of cigarettes. It was six weeks since he had promised to stop smoking, and these were the first cigarettes he had actually bought. He opened the package and offered one to the doctor, who shook his head. Trevanien, with the cigarette going between his fingers, began to feel better. The doctor's office was, he had noted, directly above a branch of the Banque Nationale de Paris. An appropriate location since his patients were no doubt the types who had a lot of money, multiple accounts hedged in a wide variety of currencies. As his father-in-law had complained the other day, what else could you do? No one could outguess the money market these days.   The doctor returned to his desk and picked up the newspaper again: "Robert Freud, known fondly to his patients as Freud, *il dottore*, is a charming mixture of English, French and Italian, one of those pan-European gentlemen who seem to be the sole civilized remnant of life before the Second World War. Robert Freud, who was

57

educated in England and France, is said to have been a favorite of his uncle, and often spent afternoons with him when he was a child. In the late 1930's, when Sigmund Freud was dying of cancer, one of his sole consolations was said to have been the frequent visits of the young nephew from Italy."

Trevanien put out his cigarette. He had heard a story that Robert Freud was called *il dottore* because of a hilarious imitation he had once done of *il duce* at a masquerade party. However, this didn't seem to be the moment to bring up that subject. Trevanien looked at his watch. Seventeen minutes after twelve.

Suddenly the door to Freud's office opened and the woman he had seen on the street was standing in the doorway. Her features were twisted and intense, as though she were making a great effort to concentrate on something impossible to remember.

"Do you want to sit down?"

"Unhh —" gasped the woman. Her hand was at her throat, on the zipper of her coat, and then she was starting to pull it down.

"Please," said Robert Freud.

Freud looked at Trevanien.

The woman had something in her hand, she was starting to throw it at the doctor, Trevanien dove forward, putting himself between Freud and the woman.

"Oh no," sighed the woman, as she released the object.

It flew across the room. Suddenly, in the center of his chest, Trevanien felt a sharp expanding pain. The intense concentration had passed from the woman's face: she was released, serene, her lips curved in a half-smile.

As Trevanien sank to the carpet he put a hand up to where he had been hit, plunged his palm into the now spreading blood which was gradually soaking through his shirt.

The woman knelt beside him. "It's so beautiful."

Trevanien withdrew his hand from his shirt. He wasn't dying. He was lying on the floor of the office of the newly-famous Robert Freud, *il dottore*, who was smiling as Trevanien explored the bag of warm blood that had exploded against the knot of his tie and was now dripping through his clothes and running down his skin.

Trevanien lay on his back in Helen Spender's bathtub. The water, steaming hot, was covered with a healthy layer of multi-colored bubbles. Attached to the ceiling was a mirror surrounded by plaster angels holding hands and playing some seraphic version of ring-around-the-rosie. According to Helen, the ceiling and various other decorations had been installed at the request of its previous occupant, a Cabinet Minister of the Interior who kept it as his Paris "nest."

"So anyway, here you are again, covered in blood. You always wanted to be a war correspondent."

In his left hand Trevanien had one of his Cuban cigars. In his right, a double vodka martini. "Things are falling apart," Trevanien said.

"Any port in a storm."

"You know that's not true. The truth is I had absolutely nowhere else to go."

"Home, George, there's always home."

"My wife is having someone over to measure her bust for a dress. I couldn't disgrace her in front of Raoul or whomever."

11 THE AFTERNOON IN THE STUDY

He was in the old man's study. Summer was long gone and the suits which had seemed so hot in August were now not warm enough. Except when he was with his uncle, because his uncle's study always had a fire and a table set with pots of tea and hot chocolate.

The old man was sleeping and while he slept Robert was standing at his desk, looking at a manuscript. His sister came into the room. Usually she stayed outside with the others. She didn't like the old man — after the visits she made jokes about the way his face looked, the trouble he had speaking, his shaking hands. Now, she came and stood across from Robert, on the other side of the desk.

"What are you snooping at?" she asked. Then she began looking in the drawers.

"Get out of here," Robert said.

"Don't be silly, he won't wake up." She had found an old-fashioned pistol — a fancy wood-inlaid duelling gun — and was waving it about. "Look at this. I bet he's going to kill himself."

"Put it back," Robert said.

"One of these days he'll point it at his brain and blow it through his ears. That will make a mess."

"I told you to put it back," Robert said. He began walking around the desk towards his sister.

"Stay away."

Suddenly Robert was aware that the old man had woken up. He turned around. His uncle was looking at them, his greenish eyes half open, a strange smile on his face. As though he were awake and dreaming at the same time.

"Did you hear what I told you?" his sister asked. She pointed the gun towards him. "He's going to blow his brains right through his ears."

Robert leapt.

12 THE PSYCHOPATHOLOGY OF EVERYDAY LIFE

Freud grasped the arms of his chair, pulled himself to his feet. He looked at the girl. She returned his stare, her face full of hate. The boy was lying on the floor. Blood was running from his cheek to the carpet. He was crying. The girl was still holding the gun. The study was filled with a cold light.

"It was an accident. My hand slipped."

Using his cane, Freud inched forward. He could feel the world growing out of his mind, the entire cosmos exploding forward on his brainwaves. He looked down at the boy. Somehow, over the past few months, he had begun to imagine that the boy would be his disciple, that after his own death the boy would become the new king, the new fleshly embodiment of truth.

Now the boy's eyes were turned towards his. Freud looked directly into the boy's pupils, willed the contents of his brain to be poured directly into the boy's.

The cane slipped and Freud fell to his knees. "Old man," he said bitterly. He took his handkerchief out of his pocket and began dabbing at the blood. Others had come into the room. The doctor had been called. The floor trembled with comings and goings. Freud knelt over the bleeding boy, muttering, muttering, no one knew what.

MOSTLY MADAME LAROUSSE

It was morning. Through his window Maurice could see the Paris sky. It was the color of frozen milk. Maurice was a writer. "The Paris sky was the color of frozen milk," he considered writing. A couple of years ago his creative writing teacher had told him that he excelled at writing descriptions of light. Light suffusing the horizon. Light caressing otherwise untouched skin. Light through which cigarette smoke drifted like slow moving fogbanks. That had been a couple of years ago, during his lyrical phase, one which made no mention of dairy products. At that time he lived in an attic with a girl called Sharon and typed all night while beer cans accumulated on his desk like little clusters of bowling pins. At dawn the light would breathe into his face and Maurice would go downstairs and have a bath before climbing into bed with Sharon who was always waiting until one morning, when she wasn't, and that was the end of his lyrical phase. The same day his creative writing professor told him about light, he also told Maurice that to succeed he would have to move to Toronto and "meet important people."

Now Maurice was living in Paris. He was sitting

67

at his desk with a blank piece of paper in his portable typewriter. Taped to the wall in front of him was the contract in which Trevanien Enterprises, Ltd., had offered Maurice an advance of ten thousand American dollars against the world rights to Maurice's novel, "an untitled book of fiction of at least one hundred thousand words hereafter referred to as 'The Work.' "

"Yellow sun filled the room," Maurice wrote, "with a hard bright light. It was cold. It was clear. Later the cold clear light would be stained by the blood of —"

For luck Maurice was wearing pants and a sweater given to him by Sharon. This was after they had gotten back together. The pants were baggy corduroy with pockets big enough for whiskey flasks and notebooks. The sweater was from Spain, a rough wool fisherman's number that, with the pants, made Sharon say that he looked like Ernest Hemingway.

"Ernest Hemingway!" Maurice had protested. "What about Canada? I could look like Mazo de la Roche or Pierre Berton."

Sharon had laughed. That day he had still wanted to make Sharon laugh. It was his post-lyrical phase — bitter humor, one-liners, scotch instead of beer. "Canada has no romance," she had finally said. "America is romantic. Paris is romantic. Remember

68

you used to say you could take me to Paris?"

Now Maurice was in Paris, but without Sharon. He had his contract. He had his novel. He had a vision of himself as a complete idiot. "Yellow sun filled the room," Maurice wrote. "The idiot lay with his arms outstretched, a death waiting to be discovered."

Without having to be told Maurice knew that Trevanien Enterprises, Ltd., would not be pleased by such a sentence. TEL was an optimistic operation. Maurice looked out the window. The frozen milk was melting at the edges. Then Maurice began to type. He was writing a novel about his neighbor Fernando, except that in his novel Fernando was a Mexican truck driver secretly carrying out Aztec death rituals. In the scene Maurice was writing, Fernando was trying to pick up an Egyptian tourist at a truck stop scene set in Palm Springs.

As he typed the sky melted and Maurice began to whistle. Hours passed. Eventually Maurice no longer knew what Fernando would do. It was time to find out. He hid his manuscript, then went to the hall and knocked at Fernando's door.

"Come in," Fernando said.

Maurice went in.

"This morning I am doing tests," Fernando said. "Help me."

More time passed. Fernando and Maurice were sitting in Fernando's hotel room. Fernando was telling Maurice that in the fields outside of a certain Moroccan village, children get stoned by running through the marijuana fields until their bodies are covered in hash oil.

"Amazing," said Maurice. Hash oil had coated his tongue, the roof of his mouth, the pink interstices between his teeth, the opening of his throat. He breathed deeply and felt the oil gurgling in his lungs. Once he had known something about lungs: their pinkness, their porous inner surfaces, their millions of tiny breathing sacs. Once he ran marathons during which he pictured the insides of his lungs industriously processing oxygen for the blood which was waiting to gurgle through his veins — feeding muscle, refreshing tissue, cheering up primitive portions of his brain. In those days Sharon would be waiting for him at the finish line.

"What do you think?" Fernando asked.

Maurice thought many things. He coughed. He listened to the voice of Madame Larousse as it curled up the winding stairs. Madame Larousse was at her post — her listening post, one might say, except that she used it for talking.

Maurice could not hear what Madame Larousse was saying. Instead he concentrated on her voice.

It was a voice like an electric razor, a voice with many different cutting edges, each one set at its own special angle.

"Madame Larousse," said Maurice.

Fernando began to hum. Then he broke off and commenced singing in a high falsetto that Maurice had never heard before:

> Blow my whistle
> Tip my caboose
> I want give my heart
> To Madame Larousse

Maurice went to the window. In the square below dozens of pigeons were walking in irregular paths, eating breadcrumbs. The crumbs were supplied by the mother of Madame Larousse. Maurice imagined himself writing home: "I am watching the mother of my concierge feeding pigeons in the square." The perfect beginning for a postcard. The problem was: who would receive it? Not his children. He didn't have any, which at the moment he considered fortunate, because the thought of children covering themselves in hash oil had sent another part of his mind plunging into depression over the ever-increasing corruption of the human consciousness, its gradual moral emptying in the face of the arms race, ecological disasters, etc. Nor could he send the postcard to his own mother, since she would take such a sentence as proof definitive that he thought she was — or soon would be — sufficiently gaga to waste perfectly good bread on disease-ridden birds. There was only one possibility. Sharon, with whom he had not communicated in three years. She alone could receive such a postcard. She alone could know what he meant. She alone believed in reciprocity. She would take his lousy crumb, transform it, send it back. Soon crumbs would be flying back and forth across the Atlantic. Soon he would be afraid to go home lest Sharon be waiting for him at the airport. Or worse: what if she dropped in? "Hi, thought I'd see if Paris really is romantic. Who's the woman at the desk with the corrugated cheeks?"

Before Maurice could think of his answer there was a knock and Madame Larousse, the woman with the corrugated cheeks, had poked her head around the door. She had a way of doing this, of presenting herself face-first, that made it appear her head was a mask carried on a stick.

"*Monsieur Maurice, on vous demande.*"

Until a month ago there had been a buzzer system connecting the front desk to the various rooms, so that when there was a telephone call for a guest, the buzzer could be sounded. Then, as Madame

Larousse had explained at the time, the establishment had decided to modernize itself. "We will be a hotel of three *étoiles*," she had concluded. This meant the subtraction of buzzers, the addition of telephones. Stage one was now concluded, stage two was in limbo.

Meanwhile, the face of Madame Larousse was hovering. Maurice stared at her frankly. He had learned, since coming to Paris, that open staring was more acceptable than furtive glances.

Madame stared back.

"*On vous demande*," repeated Madame Larousse. "*Un gentilhomme.*"

For the first time Maurice noticed that fanning out from the corners of the lips of Madame Larousse were little curtains of flesh that framed her top two chins.

Abruptly, Madame Larousse turned around. For a moment the unexpected illusion of youth: thick reddish-blonde hair falling to conceal the neck and meet the collar of her white blouse. "Madame Larousse," Maurice imagined himself exclaiming, "you lose half a century merely by turning one hundred and eighty degrees."

Clump. Clump. Clump. The slow sad footfall of Madame Larousse as she was forced to descend the steps of her own hotel. The maids were off this morning. The telephones had failed to be installed. The elevator had its own problems. Poor Madame Larousse.

"You were staring at her again," said Fernando.

"I couldn't help it."

"*Mais — on vous demande. Un gentilhomme.*"

"I go," announced Maurice. He stood up. Inside his body phantom spheres began colliding with each other. Maurice fell against the door. He straightened himself up. The mirror above Fernando's dresser accosted him. He saw his face and sucked in his cheeks. "Smooth, thin, cruel," he muttered, not very convincingly.

Absolutely, you absolutely must come to the apartment tonight." Trevanien laughs warmly. It is lunchtime at La Coupole. Maurice is eating well, but trying not to show his greed. Trevanien, of course, is paying; otherwise they would not be eating at a famous restaurant with linen tablecloths and tourists with cameras. This too was part of the contract, one of the unwritten parts. Over the telephone Trevanien had said, as always, that he had something for Maurice. Then he had suggested the restaurant and the time. "You don't mind meeting for lunch, do you? I have some work to do this afternoon."

Trevanien laughs. Trevanien's laugh is his "best feature," a perfectly calculated voyage from belly to mouth climaxing in a warm chuckle that exposes perfect teeth, then dies away quietly like a desert sunset. Maurice thinks Trevanien is the perfect American in Paris. Tallish, wide-shouldered, thick wavy hair. His button-down shirts are made of real cloth and he always has a jacket. Trevanien is President of Trevanien Enterprises, Limited. TEL is a non-profit literary and theatrical agency. The vice-President is his wife. Trevanien's wife is rich. Trevanien writes a syndicated column for an American newspaper.

"What are you working on these days?" Trevanien asks. To show this is a serious question, not simply a routine politeness, he refills Maurice's glass with the excellent wine they are using to wash down the oysters. When he first met Trevanien, Maurice would have inspected the label. That was before the rules of the game had been clarified. Now he simply accepted whatever Trevanien offered, without question, and in return Trevanien continued to offer. Not only the contract, not only the lunches in good restaurants but work. Every month or two

Maurice would "research" an article for Trevanien, for which duty Trevanien would pay him several hundred American dollars that had no relationship to income tax laws. "Research" included writing up the results in the form of a column which, Maurice suspected, Trevanien merely edited very lightly before sending in. Maurice also suspected Trevanien had an entire staff of "researchers," all expatriates like himself, all thin, all needing money.

"I mean your writing," Trevanien says.

Maurice shrugs.

"The novel," Trevanien says, "how is it going?"

"It's going," Maurice says.

"I can hardly wait to read it," enthuses Trevanien.

Maurice worries. His novel is a pile of semi-related scrawls stuffed into a cardboard carton beside the tiny desk Madame Larousse found for him. The other night, Maurice had intended to re-read them: first he stacked and counted the pages — two hundred and four — then he started reading. On page two he had fallen asleep.

To gain time Maurice sips at his wine, takes one of Trevanien's cigarettes. He sees that Trevanien's lips are quivering. This is the one chink in the armor, the chink that allows Maurice to like him. When Trevanien's mouth moves from one expression to another, there is a sudden rattling of the lips, tiny uncontrollable flashes of fear.

"I'm serious," Trevanien says.

"Are you calling in the contract?"

"Don't be silly."

"How much is a hundred thousand words?"

"Not much, once you get going."

"This is crazy."

"You need more money?"

"How about a hundred thousand dollars. Then I can get a nurse."

Trevanien shakes his head. "You don't need a nurse. You're the lumberjack type. Anyway, even for the rest of the ten thousand you have to show what you've written."

"It's not ready."

"Sight unseen, I can give you only five thousand."

"Sight unseen," Maurice repeats. "How about just unseen, or even unsighted? It's an insult to be offered money by a man who can't even talk."

"You're proud but you're desperate."

"You're married but you're weird."

"My wife wants to know why you never come to dinner. She doesn't believe you exist. She thinks I'm meeting a hooker or something."

"Or something."

"After lunch I go to the office. You know that."

Maurice nods. It is true. He has even seen Trevanien's office: a small studio apartment furnished with a bed and a desk.

"Have some armagnac," Trevanien says.

"I'm supposed to go to my French lesson this afternoon."

"Forget your French lesson. Anyway, pleasure is the real lesson of France." Trevanien beckons to the waiter, who brings them the bottle and two glasses.

T ime passed. Trevanien went in one direction, Maurice the other. It was cold and the wind was blowing fine drops of rain into his face. The hash oil Fernando tested on him had faded during the lunch with Trevanien, but now it was back, sending fiery battalions through the blood vessels of his brain, illuminating great expanses of landscape in brief brilliant flashes that receded before he could make out the details. What would Hemingway do in a situation like this? Maurice asked himself. And then, as soon as he asked the question, he knew the answer: he would walk into a bar.

Maurice walked into a bar. He pulled a newspaper out of his jacket and spread it on the table. By the time he had finished reading it, his equilibrium would have returned and he would be able to leave the bar and return to his hotel. Then, in a few hours, Fernando would come to his room and say, "What did you do this afternoon?"

"I went to a bar," Maurice would reply.

Fernando would nod, smiling. He regarded Maurice, or so Maurice believed, as a tragic figure burdened by the meaningless destiny of the gringo universe.

Maurice peered into a dark corner. He hunched his shoulders, Hemingway style. "It was cold and it was thirsty," Hemingway would have written. "It was out of season and in the corner of the hotel three naked waitresses were playing cards with three naked bullfighters. There was the sound of cardboard slapping against the scarred wood and then there was a scraping noise as a chair was pushed back."

One of the waitresses stood up. She came to Maurice's table. Hemingway had been lying: she wasn't naked at all; she was wearing a transparent plastic apron with two transparent pockets. One pocket was empty. In the other she carried her coin collection.

"Une bière," Maurice coughed out. He had been given so many pointers on how to say his French

vowels that he could no longer speak normally. Instead he barked his words and hoped to be mistaken for a peasant. Hemingway, of course, would never have resorted to anything so ridiculous. If anyone had questioned his French he would have spoken to him in Spanish. Or written a book about him saying that he was impotent.

The waitress turned around and began walking away. "Horses have tails," Hemingway might have said to Fitzgerald. It would have been just something that came into his head. Or, Maurice might have said it to Fernando, had only Fernando been there to hear it. But Fernando was at the dentist. In any case, he disapproved of Maurice barking his words. "You need to work on your presence," he had already advised.

The waitress came back with a bottle of beer. Then she returned to her card game. Other customers began drifting in. The other waitresses took turns serving them.

Maurice, on his fourth beer, began to reminisce about his time in Paris. During the past months his only sexual contact had been with the daughter of an Egyptian Embassy official who had previously been stationed in Iceland. Maurice had gotten to know her at the Alliance Française, and when she had discovered he was from Canada she had asked him to take her back to his hotel room because she was lonely for snow. "You have breasts like pyramids," Maurice had told her, and they had met several more times. Now Maurice had put her into his book. To punish her he was making her have an affair with Trevanien. While typing he could imagine them together but once out of his room the combination was hard to believe.

Maurice, after his sixth beer, yielded to the inevitable. Following the directions indicated by a series of bright yellow signs, he stumbled down a narrow twisting staircase. At the bottom of the stairs was a red-tiled anteroom featuring a sink and two doors. Above the sink was a mirror which Maurice glanced at gingerly. As he had suspected: the worst. His eyelids were at half-mast, the pouches beneath had swollen to the size of baby laundry bags. A multi-colored stubble covered his cheeks and chin.

Maurice let his eyes slide to the doors. On one was a picture of a man with a hat. That was definitely the door Hemingway would have chosen. Maurice went in and closed the door behind him.

Pitch darkness. In search of the lightswitch he began to grope at the humid tiled wall. His stomach contracted. Primal fears, unwanted smells. When he was a little boy he had once stood at the edge of a cess pit watching his father empty it. It had been a muggy summer day and Maurice had gotten sick to his stomach. Later, when his father was finished, they had gone swimming in the lake. Maurice closed his eyes tightly and tried to imagine his body sliding through the cold clean water. It didn't work. He began pushing his hand along the wall again. Then his foot hit a slippery patch. He lost his balance and fell to his knees. His brain was going berserk. The landscapes illuminated by heat lightning had become a vast and soggy battlefield of neurons in revolt against the messages they were being asked to carry. Maurice struggled to his feet. Then his hand found the switch. He turned on the light. He was in a disgusting Turkish-style lavatory with mustard-colored walls. He locked the door and proceeded to conduct himself as carefully as possible under the circumstances. The problem was, of course, that the circumstances were becoming compromised, blurred, difficult to assess. While in the bathroom he heard steps outside, then even a knock at the door. In one of his nightmares three naked matadors stomped in. They all looked like Ernest Hemingway and they were all wearing transparent plastic aprons. At that moment, squatting in a position for which there is no Olympic event, Maurice remembered another Hemingway dictum: a true man is prepared to die at all times.

Maurice waited. Death failed to arrive. There was a logic here, Maurice told himself. Death had failed to arrive because he was under the protection of Trevanien Enterprises, Ltd. Until the contract was fulfilled, he had nothing to fear. On the other hand, he also had nothing to offer. His lyrical phase was over. Equally his post-lyrical phase. Writing a novel about his friends was only a stopgap idea and, besides, his best friend Fernando was sinking ever more deeply into a state of nothingness. Nothingness, unfortunately, was not a suitable subject for a novel. Especially not a TEL novel. For that novel a story of hope, triumph and courage was required. Maurice decided to be his own best example. Maurice stood up and reassembled himself. Outside the cubicle he managed to wash his hands and face without looking at himself. Then he returned to his table for the newspaper but instead of leaving he sat down again.

"Will there be anything else?"

Maurice looked at the waitress. He became aware that once again lights were beginning to burn.

"A dim light is shining in my mind," said Maurice.

"Self-knowledge is the first step to enlightenment," replied the waitress. The dim light grew slightly less dim. Maurice realized that the waitress had spoken to him in English. He also realized that the dim light, now grown slightly less dim, had something to do with the waitress. He had, as they say, seen her before. He wondered whether to say it.

"Can I offer you a drink?" asked Maurice.

"Sure." The waitress came back with a bottle of brandy. "Why don't you offer me a glass of this?"

"You're speaking English," Maurice stuttered.

"So are you."

"The light is shining brighter," said Maurice. Now he recognized her. She was a former fine arts student, a year ahead of him.

"Let it shine, the weather has been lousy for months."

"What are you doing in Paris?"

"Some friends sent me here. It's a long story." Maurice nodded.

"I came down to the bathroom to see if you were all right," said the waitress. "Maybe I should have talked to you earlier."

The waitress drank a second glass of brandy, then told Maurice that her shift was over. Soon they were outside, walking away from the bar. When they came to a Métro the waitress seemed to expect Maurice to follow her as she descended the stairs. It became clear that their common past, such as it was, was not to be the main topic. Instead, she kept up a conversation about horse-racing, the various seasons, the times she had almost made a lot of money. In all of this there was no mention of boyfriends, but Maurice couldn't imagine a waitress going unaccompanied to the races. He also couldn't remember her name. After two changes of trains they emerged from the Métro. As they walked along the street Maurice noticed that the waitress gripped his arm and averted her eyes every time they passed a butcher shop. Finally they came to a store where the waitress went in and bought an armful of vegetables.

"I bet you're famous for your cooking," said Maurice.

"I wrote the book." When they got to her building, the waitress led the way up the stairs, walking so quickly that Maurice had to struggle to keep up.

"Here we are." Putting the groceries on a counter she went and lay down on the sofa. She beckoned to Maurice. "Sit beside me. Hold my hands."

Maurice did as he was told. He looked around. The room was filled with life-sized papier-mâché figures. Some of them were wrestling, others making love in strange positions. "Who are they?"

"Richard Burton and Elizabeth Taylor. Before the break-up, of course. Do you like them?"

"They're great," Maurice said sincerely. He tried to imagine Ernest Hemingway writing a novel about a waitress who had deserted her typewriter in order to depict the doomed love affair of two movie stars using flour, paste and strips of newspaper. He couldn't. That was the thing about Hemingway, the thing — possibly the only thing — to be admired. He had learned to live within his limitations. Maurice resolved to do the same, at the first opportunity.

"Well, Maurice, before we go any further, there is one thing I must tell you." She placed his hand on her belly. Through the cloth Maurice could feel the heat of her skin.

"Maurice, I have a terrible mental condition. You must never ask me certain questions."

Maurice nodded.

"Do you believe that I am serious?"

"I don't know," said Maurice. He had not expected his resolve to be tested so soon. "Do you have a social disease?"

"I have my problems." The waitress pulled Maurice to her and kissed him softly on the lips. Maurice closed his eyes. From now on, he was certain, everything would be different. From now

86

on he would stop waking up in a sweat. From now on he would work on his novel every day, even if it did put him to sleep. From now on he would treat Madame Larousse with the impeccable courtesy she was owed. From now on he would stop dreaming about Sharon. From now on, in sum, he would live life whole and entire; uncynical, unfazed, unencumbered he would open his arms wide and embrace whatever fate delivered to him, limited or otherwise.

"Remember what I told you?" asked the waitress.

"I remember."

"Are you hungry?"

"I'm starving."

When Maurice got back to the hotel he found Trevanien sitting on the couch with Madame Larousse and watching television. As he walked through the door they turned and looked at him expectantly.

"I've found it, I've found it," Maurice imagined himself shouting. Then leaping into the air, clicking his heels and floating through the lobby. But the magic moment passed and while the eyes of Trevanien and Madame Larousse remained fixed upon his face, Maurice began walking up the stairs.

When he reached his room the door was open. Fernando was crouched in a corner, shaving slices from a piece of hash that looked like a dark green golf ball. On his bed was the cardboard box that had contained his manuscript. The 204 pages were stacked neatly beside it.

"You should be ashamed of yourself," Maurice said to Fernando. He went on to deliver a speech on the medical and social evils of drugs and alcohol. "Furthermore," Maurice concluded, "these substances are only a method of social control. Very few effective political leaders have been drug addicts or alcoholics."

"Prove it," Fernando said.

"You're ruining your life," said Maurice. "To set an example I am going to rehabilitate myself. To begin with I pledge not to drink in the morning for a whole year. And that is only the beginning. There will be further announcements. Henceforth —"

A discreet cough interrupted. Trevanien was standing in the doorway, smiling benignly. "I've read it," Trevanien announced. "You're a genius. You'll be famous forever."

Fernando nodded. His pupils were the color of dead ashes.

When morning arrived Maurice was walking down a narrow street of which he did not know the name. He had just spent an hour in a cemetery where concrete gardens surrounded concrete graves. In the graves, stacked several deep, were the bodies of the French — men, women, children. The narrow street ended at a big street. Into Maurice's face rolled wave upon wave of choking fumes. Just the other day he had said to Fernando: "Someone could make a fortune here if the French could be persuaded to keep their cars tuned."

"Keep their cars tuned?" Fernando had queried. Fernando was Spanish.

Maurice, using his Alliance Française French, spent a long time trying to explain this concept. It was hopeless. He was reminded of another time when he had hit upon the idea of franchising self-serve launderettes to small Italian towns. The whole thing would be introduced to the public by a series of billboards featuring Sophia Loren washing her underwear. Maurice, allowing this concept to fill his mind, had realized he had hit upon the idea that would make him rich. But then either you were a businessman or you were not.

Now Maurice was wrecked. His eyes were glued open. Paris was spinning about him in grimy technicolor. Through his armpits, his groin, down his limbs, ran salty polluted sweat. Maurice came to a café and sat at a sidewalk table. Once, a few months ago, he had gotten so wrecked with Fernando that he had only gotten back to his hotel by finding a taxi and giving it his address. Now he ordered a coffee. An ounce of black sludge arrived in a thimble-sized cup. Maurice drank it down. He could feel a trail of coffee grains being laid down from throat to stomach.

"This is terrible," Maurice said. He often had moments like this, moments when he forgot why he had come to a city where he wasn't sure how to make money and people laughed at his French. He closed his eyes. His feet were hot and sore. He imagined himself in a bathtub. That would be nice. But Madame Larousse did not approve of bathing. To prevent it she made sure that hot water was available only in small quantities, preferably in the middle of the night. Maurice imagined himself sitting in a tubful of cold water. He would close his eyes and pretend the cold water was a lake. Perhaps Madame Larousse would discover him in the bath. Perhaps she would note that he had grown alarmingly thin. The prospect of being inspected in the bathtub by Madame Larousse was unappealing.

Maurice rubbed the heels of his hands into his eye sockets. This was one of his mannerisms when he was depressed. The traffic was getting heavier, the intermittent waves of exhaust were agglomerating into an inescapable tidal catastrophe. Now Maurice noticed the air darkening, and to the sound of traffic was added a new and deeper drumming.

Maurice began to hallucinate. He saw a helicopter descending. Sharon stepped out. She was wrapped in a silk Canadian flag and was holding a soft drink in her hand. Cameramen were recording her movements as she pranced about on the Parisian pavement, sniffed the air, pirouetted, tasted her drink in an ecstasy of refreshment. When the sequence was over she turned and saw Maurice watching her.

"My God, you surprised me. We were just making a commercial."

"Long time no see," was all Maurice could think of saying. He rubbed his eyes again and the entire scene was replaced by a line of buses, motors throbbing. But when he took his hands away Sharon was back.

"Would you like a ride?"

Soon they were up in the air.

"Did you miss me?" Sharon asked.

"I was going to write you a postcard."

"I missed you." They had glided past the Eiffel Tower, the Arc de Triomphe, and were now hovering above the Place de la Bastille. "The divorce went through," Sharon said. "Now I'm married to someone else."

"Are you happy?"

"Of course I'm happy, you idiot. That's why I got married. How about you?"

"I have a new girlfriend," Maurice said. "I just met her yesterday."

"That's nice." Sharon took Maurice's hands in hers, then leaned over and pressed her cheek to his. "Are you happy?"

Maurice looked down. Through the glass belly of the helicopter he could see Paris spread beneath them like a crumpled picnic blanket. "You're crazy," he said.

It was Madame Larousse who saved him. She moved his bed down to the lobby, where he lay sipping tea and eating day-old bread while in between phone calls she read to him from the encyclopaedia. After a month Trevanien was permitted to visit. He assured Maurice that the contract could be extended indefinitely; it was time to forget Hemingway and think James Joyce.

Yellow sun filled the room with a hard bright light," Maurice had written. Now, re-examining his words, he realized that the light had been emanating not from the sun, but from the muscular heart of Madame Larousse. Sun, moon, room, the entire universe remained inflated thanks to ceaseless pumping of her all-knowing and miraculous organ.

Suspended in her enigmatic syntax, he allowed his former lives to drift away. While Madame Larousse wove a cocoon of French history around them, he held hands with the waitress.

One morning Maurice emerged. He went to Fernando's room. Fernando was lying naked on top of his sheets. His collarbones protruded. There were dark shadows in the valleys hunger had gouged between his ribs. His elbows seemed too large for his thin arms.

"You need breakfast," Maurice said.

Fernando did not reply.

Maurice opened the curtains. Fernando's head stayed twisted away from him, but as Maurice approached the bed he could see that even the color of burnt hashish had drained out of Fernando's eyes. Maurice called down the stairs for Madame

Larousse. She did not bother to take Fernando's pulse. Instead she instructed Maurice to shave him. By the time the police arrived, Maurice had covered the dead man's face with lather and was finished one cheek plus his throat. Beneath his fingers the cold bristly skin of his friend moved with a strange freedom over muscle and bone.

"Light broke across the dead face of his friend," Maurice wrote later. But although a Mexican truck driver called Fernando still drove through the center of his novel, its hero had become the light: a little sun, a few stars, mostly Madame Larousse.

FINAL CUTS

1 "Bird. Charles Parker. The one and only," Helen crooned. "Hit me, Bird." Out from a jumble of piano notes a long mellow line wound about them, a four-speaker electronic snake circling inside the car. They were driving across Paris. Suddenly Helen switched off the sound and opened the windows.

"What?"

"It stopped raining."

Trevanien put his foot on the brake.

"What?"

"You said it stopped raining." He got out of the car. It had been raining for a hundred, a thousand, possibly a million hours. It had been raining for so long his entire rotation of shoes was soaked and the lining of his overcoat smelled like dead mice. Or maybe that was going too far. In fact he had deleted that line from his latest newspaper dispatch. In Paris, the prospect of smelling a dead mouse was unpleasant, but far from the worst you could come up with. At home, in the hypothetical newspaper universe where he played the role of a very minor star, only visible enough to be paid, there was no place for such an odor.

It was night. Across the street a huge yellow RENAULT sign shone into the darkness. Above him rattled the Métro. He realized he was standing near the old Vélodrome, the place used for rounding up undesirables at the beginning of the Occupation.

When he had first started reading about the war, he had tried to imagine how it would have been for him in Paris, whether he would have been rounded up, whether he would have been a saint or melted into the background, who among his French friends would have turned out to be real friends, who less.

After he told Helen about this she replied, "Well, you live in Paris now."

"So?"

"So what are you? Saint or sinner? Brave man or coward?"

"Neither. Things are different."

"Are they?" And then looked at him for a moment as though he were a complete idiot and somehow missed the obvious reality that Paris was a city at war.

He reached for a cigarette. At this moment, with the train roaring over his head, bathed in the yellow light of the repair shop, the sound of Helen's heels clicking slowly towards him, Paris seemed the opposite of a city at war. It seemed perfectly, utterly, helplessly itself. Big, grimy, busy, pulsing with ten million people all thinking about the next thing they were going to eat or drink.

Or perhaps that also was going too far. Although he had voiced just that opinion a few days ago on a radio broadcast. As that thought slid through his brain Trevanien had two simultaneous revelations. The first was that his mind had begun to mimic Robert Freud's speech: "*As I said to a patient just the other day*," was a typical Freud gambit. The second was that the cigarettes he was reaching for were missing, that he must have left them on the desk of the good doctor himself.

"These two things should be connected."

"How?" asked Trevanien, startled.

"I don't know," Helen said. In her mouth was one of her own cigarettes, and she was holding up her gold lighter. Its top had become unhinged from the base. Trevanien leaned closer. He had given her the lighter in the old days, when they first met each other. When her hair was long and flowed like pale honey onto her bare shoulders, and her bright blue eyes kept searching his out, then turning away. That was before they had started sleeping together, a foreplay of long drunken lunches when it always seemed their heads, mouths armed with cigarettes, were weaving across the table in search of a light. "Here," Trevanien said the day he bought the lighter. Fifteen hundred French francs. Pale gold, almost too small for his own palm. Where he'd go from there he didn't know but found himself saying, as the gift fell from his hand to hers, "We could try one of those hotels where they don't count your suitcases."

"We'll bring shopping bags," Helen said, and for a moment he wasn't sure if she was surrendering or just raising the stakes. They bought wine, brandy, flowers. Unpacked in a room on the top floor of a stone-faced hotel on the Rue de Seine. Starting drinking as though they were still at lunch, this time out of big hotel glasses that had been wrapped in paper to prove they were clean.

I'm an American in Paris, Trevanien kept saying to himself, but he couldn't seem to get started. Helen leaning towards him. He was already married to Sandy, but Helen in those days had been single and always seemed to him like an attractive but anxious bird looking for a place to settle. Do something, Trevanien urged himself. Finally, the bottle of brandy half gone, Helen excused herself to use the bathroom. *Do something*. And then inspiration struck. He did something. In the space of a blink he kicked off his shoes and jumped into bed. Before another thought could arrive he was under the covers and breathing hard, trying not to giggle.

The next thing he knew the ocean surf was relentlessly pounding the inside of his skull. He opened his eyes. It was dark. He slid his hand across the bed. Empty. But when he sat up and looked across the room, he saw Helen in the armchair, calmly smoking and watching him.

2 Freud contemplated his naked body. Surrounded by a few millimeters of cloth, cushioned by the Recamier on which his patients lay to offer him their dreams, his body was suspended directly above the vault of his downstairs neighbor, the Banque Nationale de Paris. Just as, according to his uncle, every individual human being was doomed to repeat the psychological history of all humanity, so did each bank vault recapitulate the trials and triumphs of civilization. Inside those shining walls were to be found the stacks of bills in multiple currencies. Some from countries that had ceased to exist. The legacy of the skilled craftsman's hand in the form of necklaces, rings, unmounted jewels. The pure precious record of greed and insecurity, empires won and lost, in coins of all shapes and sizes, in stamped bars, in misshapen lumps that were the last remains of late-night meltdowns. The marriage documents, the leases, the wills. The stocks, the bonds. The marriage documents.

Marriage and banks, sex and money. These were the partnerships you could count on. Where the tender psyche and its fear of death found shelter in the comfort of multiple locks and reinforced steel walls. Hundreds of times he had given this advice to patients under duress. Why not? He, impoverished, had been attracted by a wealthy woman. Others might as well travel this same useful road.

Now he realized that before Clarissa he had never truly understood the equation. Never truly experienced it. He had thought of money as something one of the partners possessed. A big bank account, rich parents, a house, more. Physical assets that existed apart from the possessor. The way his wife had had money.

But Clarissa didn't simply *have* money. She was literally soaking with it. The very pores of her skin were impregnated with the luxurious perfumes and exotic fragrances of money. Her thick hair was lush with the oil of old wealth. Her ear lobes elongated by the weight of small perfect gemstones. "She's having surgery again," Eleanour used to say disdainfully about her sister. "That English husband of hers sends her off to have her body re-made as though she were some kind of car." A Jaguar. A Lamborghini or a Porsche. Something sleek, powerful, seamless.

"Haven't you ever heard of feminism?" Clarissa once asked when she caught Freud gaping at her. "You're not supposed to regard women as sex *objects*."

"How about sex *queens*?"

"Out of the mouths of babes," Clarissa murmured.

Freud found the bait easy to resist. This whole thing about men oppressing women just annoyed him. Anyway, speaking of who oppressed whom, Eleanour always borrowed his razor to shave her legs. Then she left it on the edge of the bathtub, its blades coated with dozens of tiny spikey hairs, some of which had grown alarmingly coarse and gray.

Clarissa, so far, kept her cosmetic secrets to herself. Although she liked to display herself, and to advantage, stretched out on the bed in the late afternoon half-light. The horizon of her body was a

lock of dark hair, a quizzical smile, an upturned
nipple, a long slow curve of belly, hip and haunch,
a leg bent into an upside-down V. And yet Freud
knew what Clarissa was trying to say. That she
wasn't simply a body, even an exquisitely formed
one on which his mouth and fingers had discovered
only a few small creases that might be the lasered
remains of surgical scars. Inside that body, informing
it, directing it, interlocking with it in a complex
web he could sense but not entirely decipher, was
a mind, the mind of Clarissa Jones, his wife's sister,
herself the wife of an Englishman who had decamped
to a separate residence for reasons Clarissa darkly
hinted at.

That move had not taken place so easily. There
had been numerous long late-night phone calls
between the sisters, unannounced visits to Paris
when Clarissa showed up, sometimes drunk, sometimes strangely late in the evening.

One afternoon she had called him at the office to
say she was at the apartment. "Eleanour went to
the hairdresser," Freud said. "I didn't know she
was expecting you."

"Maybe it's you I need to see," Clarissa said,
then laughed before Freud could reply.

When he arrived home, Eleanour was in the
bedroom, changing. Clarissa was installed in the

living room, sitting in one of those tightly uphol-
stered satin chairs that always looked to Freud like
a seventy-year-old woman in a girdle. When he
married, Freud had considered himself lucky to get
such a beautiful wife. She'd had a certain
wholesomeness about her. He had liked to admire
her in the bath, from the back, watching the play
of muscles across her shoulders, the slow graceful
movements of her neck. She was, Freud had thought
at the time, like an elegant bird, a long-necked
English bird wrapped in a woman's skin.

But over the years his wife had evolved; the bird
in the water had become a thick-skinned neuter
slopping through the mud of time. Meanwhile the
younger sister had ·grown from an awkward and
uncertain girl into a woman with polish. Not a polish
that Freud had ever before admired. In fact he had
always thought Clarissa, with her fancy earrings, her
glossy mouth, her husky laugh that reminded him
too obviously of the movies, not only unattractive
but almost repellent. The half-repulsive shell of the
exotic insect that hypnotizes you once you enter its
circle.

"I wanted to make you a proposition," she said.
"I thought, since we've known each other all these
years, that maybe you would be the right person
for me to talk to."

At that moment Eleanour reappeared, ready to go to the restaurant. But Clarissa was waiting for his answer, her head cocked slightly to one side. Freud realized that she was actually listening. That she didn't know what was going to happen.

In the middle of the night he had woken up, unpleasantly aware of having drunk too much. Eleanour, in bed beside him, was sleeping deeply, each breath throwing out a long nasal snore going all the way back to the days of the Pharoahs.

He put on his robe, crossed the hall to the bathroom. And then, on his way back, heard a strange noise. He went into the living room to investigate. Clarissa was lying on the sofa, weeping. He knelt beside her, placed a hand on her shoulder. She turned to him. In the half-light of the street lamp her face was slick with tears, her eyes glowing. For a long time, it seemed to Freud, for a time longer than he had ever known, they looked at each other. Afterwards he could not have said if she opened her arms to him or simply failed to turn away; if he had climbed up to her or just some-how —

"Don't wait," she said. And with a movement of her hand, one of her long nails so sharp against the inside of his thigh he thought she must have sliced him open, he was transplanted.

3 Freud stood at his window. Two nights ago, an arctic cold front had sent temperatures plunging. Now, on the building across the street, water from the previous week's rain had frozen on the stone window ledges, in the over-wrought cornices, dripped in long stalagmites from the tile roof. Onto all this ice the bright sun was shining, and sending a million diamond reflections straight into Freud's office.

It was early afternoon but he already could feel fatigue pulling on the skin of his face, pressing his gray metal-frame glasses down onto the bridge of his nose. Freud, *il dottore*, removed his glasses and rubbed his eyes. The world might be dancing with light, but such pyrotechnics left the doctor unmoved. Why? he asked himself. Of course he knew the answer. He *was* the doctor after all, no ordinary doctor, not even an ordinary nephew of Sigmund Freud. He was the heir, the long-silent dauphin who after years of apparent exile was now revealed to be moving inexorably towards a coronation. Four months ago his ground-breaking paper *Throwing Blood: Notes On the Neurotic Relationship between Menstruation and Art* had won him an invitation to address the British Royal Society. Even now he could see himself standing before his colleagues in the large wood-panelled hall, feel the warm tides of acceptance and success washing over him, hear the echo of his own voice as he leaned towards that huge mass of intently curious faces looking up at him as though he were Moses, his chromosomes the burning bush from which he must stagger forth with the immortal message.

The doctor turned from the window, looked morosely at his desk. Homework! He thought he had escaped it forever. But now he had that old homework feeling, the heavy nightmare of long division and Latin translation.

Stacked neatly in the center of his desk were four square-backed notebooks with hard black pebble-grained covers. Each set of covers imprisoned 192 pages, every page had 29 horizontal blue lines cut by a vertical red margin down the left hand side. Otherwise the books were nothing but blank space, waiting. Waiting, waiting.

It had all seemed so simple in Clarissa's arms. In the sweet dark hours after his triumph at the Royal Society, she had whispered to him that he was not only her prince but Sigmund Freud's as well.

At first Robert had taken this statement lightly. Clarissa, after all, was his wife's sister and so he presumed she meant that like his uncle he kept his infidelity in the family. But as the night wore on he discovered that his own body, despite its fifty-six years, still contained its own fireworks. How could he have forgotten sex? Real sex. Real clawing need. Incredible frenzy. Strange moans. The burnt-flesh smell of utter exhaustion.

"You," Clarissa whispered portentously. He was in her arms. Transplanted, transported, transfixed. "You could, you must, leave the world a legacy. Like your uncle. Surely you must see that is your destiny."

"I must," Robert Freud echoed. Although in fact he had always seen himself as merely a single-layered charlatan — on the outside the mask of respectability in the image of his uncle, on the inside a timid young medical student who for lack of better ideas had decided to use his famous name and physical resemblance to his uncle to make himself a niche to hide in. But perhaps he had sold himself short. Or discarded his old short self during a fire sale he hadn't realized he was attending. Now he was the lover of the beautiful Clarissa. Now he was the impeccably pedigreed Parisian analyst who had delivered a successful paper to the British Royal Society. Now he was a counsellor to the bored bourgeoisie whose clientele had moved beyond wealthy social-climbing expatriates to actual artists and writers. And why not? Had not his uncle interviewed Herman Hesse? Nietzsche? Had he not psychoanalysed Leonardo da Vinci and even Moses while they lay not on his couch but in their graves? Still, it was one thing to analyze dead patients, it would be another to cure them.

Freud walked to his bookshelves and picked out his uncle's work on Moses. He found a bookmark at the page with the underlined sentence: "How we who have little belief envy those who are convinced of the existence of a Supreme Power." As a student, Robert Freud had underlined those words because he thought his uncle was expressing jealousy over the fact that the world still contained billions of ignoramuses who believed in God instead of him. Now he had a new idea: that his uncle had belittled God in order to substitute reason. What an ingenious way to get out of being Jewish! Although in the end, it hadn't worked.

In any case he, Robert Freud, had rejected both religion and reason. He was neither a Jew nor a scientist. He was, he realized with a sudden flush of triumph, nothing at all, just a perpetual foreigner wearing a three-piece suit and inhabiting an office above a bank.

"*J'accuse*," Robert Freud shouted happily and threw the book across the room. It bounced off the door and landed in a tangle of pages. "*J'accuse. J'accu* —"

The telephone rang.

Freud listened to his recorded message.

Good day. You have reached the office of Robert Freud. Kindly leave a message after the tone or communicate by mail.

This message was repeated in French, then German. Another of Clarissa's ideas. "You must go international and English is the universal language." She had permitted him to follow the English with French, for that part of his clientele not yet globalized, on the condition that he conclude in German to give himself a scholarly touch. "Why not Italian?" he'd asked. "I am, after all."

"You're also married," she pointed out.

"I know you're there," his wife's voice accused. "And this time I have the information I need. Consider yourself a ruined man, *mon cher*."

Freud collapsed onto his couch. Here he was, writing a book that would change the course of world history — "Your uncle did it, surely you can too" — and his wife could offer no more help than reading him lines out of some old detective novel. *Consider yourself a ruined man, mon cher.* How else had he ever considered himself? Especially since he had married her. That was his whole problem, didn't she know? Even in the bible Jacob had been allowed an extra sister after fourteen years of hard labor. "You have to believe in yourself," Clarissa had insisted, "the way I believe in you." When she said that he felt little baby fingers reach inside his chest and touch his heart. But in retrospect he had begun to wonder exactly *how* she believed in him. Surely she hadn't spent half a lifetime at cosmetic surgeons just to fling her re-made self at her sister's husband. He might be transplanted but she was merely in transit. Anyone could see that, even a specialist on the psychological meaning of menstruation.

His telephone rang once more. When Freud's trilingual message was finished his wife first insulted him, then advised him that if he didn't contact her within the hour she would call a *bricoleur* to have the lock changed on their apartment. Nor did she fail to remind him of certain details of their marriage contract that reflected the fact that their financial start in life had come from her money, not his.

Robert Freud, for the first time in three months, responded to his wife. "I'll be there right away," he announced. As he passed by his kitchenette he opened the tiny bar refrigerator and took out the bottle of champagne he'd procured for this occasion, and before hailing a taxi he bought 200 francs worth of flowers from the shop around the corner.

4

Lunch at the Zodiac Café had been a blur of activity, animal parts, inane conversations alternating with table wine, grain liquor, and even the occasional pot of tea delivered to some poor soul under doctor's orders. The comings and goings, the urgent shaking of hands, the sounds of revolution from the kitchen: all these and more had been witnessed by George Hinton Trevanien.

He had watched. He had listened. He had noted. But aside from two slowly downed beers, he had not partaken.

Now afternoon had fallen. *L'après-midi*. Like the *après-guerre* it could be regarded as a historical turning point, when the wounds and conflicts of the old gave way to peace and harmony. In the French *après-midi*, Trevanien had always thought, like in the French *après-guerre*, the lion lay down with the lamb.

This was why the Café Zodiac was now held in the grip of an unhealthy emptiness. This was why Madame Bovary had slept with men not her husband.

The afternoon. *L'après-midi*. The peace after the war. But most humans were unsuited for peace, true peace, which was why most crimes were committed in the unbearable gap between lunch and supper. Crimes of sex and embezzlement, for example, are known to be almost exclusively committed as bankers' hours draw to a close.

Trevanien, who had been sitting on a bar stool, stood up and leaned against the oak counter. The thought of banker's hours reminded him of Helen's husband, an intense banker who was always cracking his knuckles. Unlike Sandy, the other deserted spouse, his own wife. Last night she'd come into the kitchen at two in the morning and caught him making and eating pancakes. Fourteen, in all, each as perfectly round as Trevanien could manage, three to a pan, each covered lightly in applesauce and striped with genuine New England maple syrup a friend had bought for him at the American store in Berlin.

"So that's when you eat," Sandy said.

Trevanien just nodded. Sugar and starch were what he needed. His Swedish doctor, his personal physician and source, had advised him to supply his system with these items. He had also been amazed when he heard Trevanien was going to Dr. Robert Freud for a psychological cure of his addictions. "You're not *addicted*," his Swedish doctor had said. "Your problem is that your life is empty."

Sandy had been wearing a thick white terry cloth robe that made her look comfortable and secure. She'd watched Trevanien for a while, helped herself to one of Trevanien's pancakes, heated up some milk into which she mixed chocolate Ovaltine.

In the afternoon, so far as Trevanien knew, Sandy confined herself to two types of criminal activity. One was shopping. The other was doing good works. She visited female artists from whom she bought paintings and for whom she was always arranging shows at various little galleries where she was considered a valuable client.

Trevanien, leaning against the bar of the Café Zodiac, withdrew a cigarette from his pocket. His life was empty, he took drugs. His mouth was empty, he smoked cigarettes. Although officially, as part of a promise to Sandy, he was still a non-smoker. A former smoker. A successful member of the anti-tobacco crusade that would filter soot from the world's lungs and make children's lives worth living.

"I never knew you could make pancakes," Sandy said.

"I'm just a woodsman at heart."

"Have you ever thought of moving back?" And she asked this so calmly, leaning with her back against the cupboard and sipping Ovaltine, that Trevanien had almost missed what she was telling him. Which was not only that she smelled the cigarette smoke on his clothes, but that she knew about the afternoons with Helen, the evenings, what he really did when he said he had to go to his office to finish an article.

And so, though his mouth was half full of pancake, Trevanien had been forced to receive certain items of knowledge. First, that Sandy knew about Helen. Second, that his relationship to Helen was making Sandy unhappy. Third, that she would tell him this but force the issue no further. Fourth, that there was something stubborn inside him that refused to give Helen up, no matter what.

For example, at this very moment Trevanien was at the Café Zodiac not simply to meditate on crime in the afternoon, but to meet the woman herself, Helen, his mistress, possibly the love of his life, at least a woman he'd known for a long time. He'd come early because the events of last night had made him think he should reconsider everything. But instead he had only been smoking cigarettes and drinking beer. Also, it must be admitted, riding a calm sea induced by pills given to him by his Swedish physician. And, of course, waiting for Helen.

"Helen, but not of Troy," Trevanien said aloud to himself. Then shook his head. Not that his speaking aloud mattered here. Despite its trendy name, the Café Zodiac was the kind of place where the *plat du jour* was tripe three times a week, sweetbreads the rest, that is, the kind of café where you could speak English without fear of being understood. Trevanien looked at his watch. Lit a new cigarette. As he bent towards the match a shard of light got behind his aviator sunglasses and speared his left pupil. He felt a jagged bolt of lightning inscribe itself on his optic nerve.

"Substance abuse," Trevanien said to himself, but this time not aloud. This was an excellent omen. It showed unconscious control, a momentary triumph of good behavior, the possibility of making it through the rest of the day without further disaster.

Trevanien began to feel more cheerful. Last night Sandy had been depressed and suspicious. But today was today. He wondered if there might be time to spend a few discreet moments in the washroom before Helen's arrival. He imagined himself locked in the stall, hastily snuffling white powder from his palm. It was a degrading image, but life itself was degrading. His legs began to tremble and he felt a wave of self-hate. He took off his sunglasses, rubbed his eyes, put them back on. He was supposed to be overcoming, not feeding, his addiction. Life, on the other hand, was not only degrading but short. He consulted his watch. If Helen had not arrived in exactly ten minutes, he would be permitted to go downstairs. He set the alarm on his watch, shaving off two minutes for good behavior. He was about to award himself another six minutes when he saw Helen walking towards him.

He was at the bar. There were about a dozen tables on this side of the café, small round tables that could hold four people at lunch but were now, in mid-afternoon, deserted except for two at the window which had bored-looking student types with scarves wrapped around their necks.

The wind had reddened Helen's face and her eyes were glowing. She gave him a smile, the kind he used to believe carried a hidden message — that she saw what he was but didn't care. In those days the lines radiating from the corners of her eyes were invisible in the afternoon. As was the wedding ring that now winked at him as she pulled off her gloves. On the other hand, his hand, in those days he didn't worry about rushing down to the bathroom to take drugs while he was waiting for her. "Have I ruined your life?" he suddenly wanted to ask her. But of course he hadn't. She had her Belgian banker husband who seemed to spend most of his time in Strasbourg. She had her perfectly coiffed hair. She had an apparent willingness to spend limitless time with George Hinton Trevanien. He'd had no effect on her at all.

"Cold."

"A drink?"

"Could I survive their brandy?"

"Worse," Trevanien said, still thinking about the fact she had so easily survived him.

She took out her cigarettes, looked down at his. "I thought you quit."

"Started again. Therapy. Infantile regression. You know the rant."

"I can't imagine you actually on the couch. What do you say?"

Trevanien looked away from her, ordered brandy for Helen, the same for himself. Soon they were sitting at one of the round tables, glasses in hand, tilting towards each other. Trevanien closed his eyes and was certain he could feel her breath on his face; also the little hyphen in his nervous system that was like a child in the dark, reaching out with both hands for something to hold onto.

"You know," Helen said, "sometimes I feel we've made ourselves a little nursing home in the center of our lives. Do you ever talk to your doctor about that?"

"No."

5 Robert Freud, nephew of the immortal Sigmund, was lying on his own couch. Through his office window filtered the dark light of constant rains. For the past three weeks, since the episode at his wife's apartment when she had dropped the bottle of champagne out the window and they had both watched, equally amazed, as it accelerated towards the sidewalk, Freud had adopted a second skin, a set of luminescent turquoise silk long underwear. This was a gift from Clarissa. Over the silk he armored himself in his customary dark three-piece wool suit, a high-collared shirt and the diagonally striped gold, maroon, and navy blue tie that was supposed to send off a generic private school signal. At least that had been his wife's idea. To Freud, the stripes — like Neapolitan ice cream — stood for the layers of the mind.

"Ego, superego, id," Freud now intoned. Not for the first — or the hundredth — time that morning. "Ego, superego, id. Ego, superego, id."

Since the champagne had exploded up from the cement, these words had become his mantra. Thousands of times a day he chanted it, hoping to unlock the Muse and release the book that would change the world. "You'll dedicate it to me," Clarissa whispered. Meanwhile, she had announced that in order to avoid sapping his creative powers, she was withholding her favors until he produced the first chapter.

The first chapter! So far he had yet to find the first word. Lists, outlines, notebooks filled with useful quotations — he had tried everything. Including — again following the immortal Sigmund? — some cocaine he had obtained from George Trevanien, the American who came to him for treatment of his addictions.

"Ego, superego, id." He had repeated the mantra over and over — spoken it, barked it, sung it — but to no avail. He closed his eyes. His beard felt itchy and his nose was running. This was cocaine? This was the magic drug that had brought his uncle immortality? He closed his eyes. His eyelids lay heavily on his cheeks, like stone lions sleeping outside a bank. Now they were starting to tremble as though they were about to spring upon some unsuspecting passerby. Fountains of light played across his field of vision. It made him think of Cecil B. de Mille's

The Ten Commandments. There was a real movie. Unlike the last movie he had seen with his wife, an arty American bore which consisted of watching people smoke cigarettes. Now a picture of his wife floated majestically into his mind. Cleopatra on her barge, she was wearing a low-cut dress and standing on a stage. She opened her mouth and began to sing, silently. The lions considered leaping down her throat. He could hear her voice, or at least a whisper. "All right," Freud said, "tell me anything you want. Get it off your chest. Speak your mind. Forget I am your estranged husband. Think of me as your doctor, the way you used to." And then suddenly he remembered something long forgotten, that when he and Eleanour used to make love in that first year after their marriage, she liked him to pretend he was a doctor, examining her for the first time. "Look more carefully, are you sure there's nothing?" she would insist as he explored her. The voice she used in those moments was timid and soprano, the voice of herself as a little girl, pretending.

Freud suddenly stood and crossed the room to his desk. Beside the notebooks was a package of Marlboro cigarettes. After each of his visits Trevanien always left behind his cigarettes, claiming his new drug-free life was about to begin.

Freud picked up the package and looked at the

cowboy. How comfortable it would be to be mounted on a horse, riding serenely through a white nowhere. He took out a cigarette and sampled its fit between his fingers. There was a look on the cowboy's face, a white nowhere look that wasn't entirely convincing. Like Trevanien's white nowhere look. The American journalist had a handsomely cut face, an air of total assurance, yet he was nothing but a miserable child. Freud's own face flashed into his mind: the beard he had grown to hide the scars from the time his sister shot him; the sallow tint of his skin; the way his eyes were sometimes too close together, others too far apart; the tightly drawn lines of worry and boredom. Thank God I don't have to look at my own face, Freud thought.

As he lit George Trevanien's cigarette he was suddenly and unexpectedly seized by a sad, pocked feeling. That the universe was incomplete, holes everywhere, little emptinesses where love should be. Time turned backwards. The holes grew larger, darker, began to streak into deep canyons of regret. His heart pinched. Then he realized he was experiencing not sorrow over the past, but the initial stages of a heart attack which would leave him gasping on the floor, clutching the first cigarette he had smoked in eighteen years.

Freud stared at his desk, at the notebooks waiting

to be filled. The way his sister had stared at his uncle's desk the afternoon she shot him. Then he had a sudden unwanted flash of what Sigmund Freud would think him. A fool. Why not? He would never fill those pages. Never again get inside the circle of Clarissa's love. He might as well go back to his wife. Confess, apologize, grovel.

Freud inhaled. His lungs locked on the tobacco, as though they had been waiting for it, outstretched the whole eighteen years. He exhaled. Smoke streamed from his mouth. He was on horseback. And then, without his having to will it, the horse began to move. When he turned to wave goodbye only Clarissa was there to see him leave. Then his brain stem pulsed and he was finally admitted into the perfect eternity of the great white nowhere.

6 In March the weather broke. Warm Mediterranean winds swirled up the coast, across the massif central, took the wintry blue out of the Paris skies and replaced it with a soft pearly glow that sent Freud out of his office and into the streets. He would walk quickly, breathing deeply, rushing with no particular destination, feeling spring must be hidden somewhere close by. During the day, between appointments, he sometimes took the Métro to the Luxembourg Gardens. There he paced more slowly, weighing the rhythm of his steps, looking for signs of budding leaves and watching the gardeners with their ungloved hands plunged into the soil. The light was lasting longer now. One morning he forgot to put on the silk underwear Clarissa had given him. All day his skin felt strangely alive and liberated. In the evenings he began making long sorties into sections of Paris he hadn't visited for years. When dark came he would pick a restaurant at random, order his steak and a small carafe of red wine, then take a taxi back to his office.

There, by the light from a single green-shaded lamp, he would examine the empty pages of his notebooks. All need to write in them had gradually dissipated. Now it was simply enough to gaze at the receding white space. After which, tired and satisfied with his day, he would pull out a small sofa bed his wife had once stuck in a corner of his office because she didn't want to throw it out, change into his single set of pyjamas, and go to sleep.

On a certain day near the end of the month, rain, then a phone call from his wife's lawyer, stopped him from going out. Just after he was finished on the telephone, Trevanien arrived. That evening, an evening during which the sky turned a spectacular neo-April blue-gold, Freud, seated at his desk, found that his hand moving trance-like and of itself had just written two words on the highest of the twenty-nine blue horizontal lines on the first page of the first notebook.

Little Sisters.

Only a few hours ago, Trevanien had talked to him about his little sisters. Twins. Lying on the Recamier, stocking feet folded one over the other, Trevanien had sobbingly confessed he had once fantasized about going to bed with them.

"And so?"

"What do you mean, *and so?* Doctor, I'm telling you I wanted to go to bed with my twin sisters, both at once."

"Dry your eyes, Mr. Trevanien. Please. I can assure you that nothing is more normal than the desire to go to bed with sisters."

"Doctor, you've got to be kidding."

"Believe me, Mr. Trevanien, on the continent it is the accepted thing."

"Really? I never realized that."

"Perhaps people don't speak as freely to you as they do to me."

Trevanien had looked at him, torn between doubt

and relief. Freud looked back. He wondered if he really wanted this man in his office. "Mr. Trevanien, has it ever occurred to you that you might be wasting your money here?"

For the hours since Trevanien's departure the Doctor had sat rooted to his chair, totally immobilized, this due to the white powder Trevanien had spread out in several lines on the glass-topped desk.

For the whole time he'd been in a tunnel, a tunnel with a white light at the end, a white light that sometimes exploded into the whole universe, others dimmed and faltered. Now his hand had moved and the tunnel had gone away. This must mean, Freud deduced, that he had arrived. He had dismounted into a world of total serenity, a world made up of two words, *Little Sisters*, the memory of his life as it had been before he passed through the tunnel, whatever happened from this moment on.

Freud closed his eyes. He saw Trevanien sitting behind a table of a smoky nightclub. Beside him, her chair close enough that their shoulders touched and their thighs ran together was Helen. A shiny-haired, strangely eager-looking woman whose picture Trevanien had shown him.

Helen was squinting in the darkness, looking closely at the drummer, a dreadlocked albino whose face was sucking up the glow from the spotlight. Helen squeezed Trevanien's shoulder. Trevanien leaned closer to Helen. Inside Trevanien's skull now, Freud looked through Trevanien's eyes at Trevanien's hand as it slid towards his drink. Freud could feel his thirst, a dry anxiety that kept accelerating in unwanted counterpoint to the drumming.

Helen's hand was in his now. Trevanien wanted to close around it. A few days ago, standing outside the car, bathed in the golden RENAULT sign, Trevanien had wondered if he might be falling in love with Helen.

"We could go right now," Helen said.

Freud felt the jolt as it hit Trevanien. A flame through his nervous system that ignited his belly, his chest, sent a long white flare up through his spine, turning the inside of his skull white liquid crystal. And then there was the loud blast of a saxophone ripping through the universe, an exploding jet of need and desire, and Freud was again staring at his page.

In the morning Freud had no memory of falling asleep. He awoke, his head on the desk, lying beside the notebooks he had filled before losing consciousness. When he stood up, Freud felt not the colossal

aching hangover he expected, but a rush of exhila-
ration and youth, the way he used to feel when he
rose, weeping, from his own analyst's couch and
rushed down the narrow stairs to the crowded
streets, eager to join humanity, tears still streaming
down his face . . .

In the kitchenette he set up the automatic coffee
system, then went to the bathroom where he
showered and changed into a clean shirt in prepa-
ration for his meeting with the lawyer and his wife.

At this meeting he was supposed to be signing
the separation agreement that would lead to the
gradual disentanglement of his and his wife's affairs;
that is, his impoverishment. But she wouldn't be
able to starve him into submission. Thanks to some
creative book-keeping he had hidden much of his
income both from his wife and the internal revenue
department. Not such a difficult trick: it only
involved a two-tiered schedule of fees, the first to
be paid by cheque, the second in cash. A little
sous-table the French called it, but everyone did it
in the open. Some of his unofficial profits were in
a safety deposit box in the vault below his office.
The rest had been converted into a condominium
in the Swiss Alps along with a few accessory
precautions.

When his toilet was completed, Freud drank his

coffee, had a glass of orange juice from the carton he kept in his bar refrigerator, then went outside. Black rain-filled clouds loomed over the city but Freud hummed as he walked, breathing deeply, unable to resist happily rubbing his hands together. From the open door of a bakery came the fragrance of fresh bread and croissants. Freud, unable to resist, bought a still-warm *pain au chocolat*. As he bit into its center, the chocolate literally melted in his mouth. Why not? Why shouldn't chocolate melt in his mouth? It was a sign he would be persuasive. And persuasive he would need to be, because he had decided that at the lawyer's office he would beg his wife's forgiveness, implore her to give him one more chance, and propose a one-month courtship after which, if she were satisfied, they would resume their conjugal life.

To overcome her resistance and seal the bargain, he planned to get down on his knees and crawl across the floor. When he arrived at Eleanour's lap he would present her with the ring he had bought for Clarissa. At this very moment the ring was in his pocket, riding in a velvet-lined box that had once been its ship of destiny and was now its coffin. His coffin. Unless, of course, he relented and changed his mind. Anything was possible.

Freud stopped at a traffic light. *Was* anything

possible? Was it really possible he could step out of his old self, leave it frozen at this corner traffic light, and walk away a free man? Was *anything* possible? Could a completely unexpected event really intervene and change his life? Or was he simply marching to the inevitable? Behind the sweet taste of the melted chocolate lurked a bitter aftertaste. The truth was that unless some unpredicted asteroid knocked his planet off course, a few hours or days or weeks from now he would be back in the old bedroom, watching Eleanour sitting in her slip at her dressing table, her round dowager shoulders slumped forward as she peered into the mirror. Freud's palms filled with the sensation of Eleanour's cold grainy skin. They began to sweat. He clapped them nervously together, then rubbed his eyes. For a brief moment he saw Trevanien as he had been in the middle of last night, Trevanien in Helen's bed, Trevanien guiltily suspended over the half-satisfied body of his mistress.

The image faded. He opened his eyes. Crossing the street towards him, wearing a tight red skirt that made her legs cross in front of her as she walked, was an elderly woman with a copy of *Le Figaro* tucked beneath her elbow. The woman, holding one arm in front of her, was being led by a tiny beige terrier. Her face was screwed into an expression of permanent distaste. The dog's little legs were bouncing as its tiny claws made their scratchy rebounds off the pavement. Its bright ratty eyes surveyed the terrain for tasty morsels.

The sun had found a narrow splintering gap between the clouds and was shining straight into the woman's face. She didn't see Freud coming. Nor, Freud realized, could she see the other woman. This one was approaching from the right. In a loose-fitting jogging suit with big red and yellow horizontal stripes, she was riding a bicycle, not a fancy racing machine but a swaying fat-tired dinosaur, big front basket overflowing with bags filled at the nearby street market.

Freud raised his umbrella. The dog swung its head towards the approaching bicycle.

Fat-tires-jogging-suit was close enough for Freud to see that she had freckles on her face, freckles on the backs of her plump ringless fingers. "You've got freckles instead of rings," Freud imagined himself intoning. "And you think this is a coincidence? Madame, what we have here is a symptom, one from which your entire condition can be deduced. If you'll permit me, Madame."

"*Mesdames*," he shouted aloud. "*Attention*. Stop." But neither lady responded. Seconds later they were both lying on the road and the dog was yapping.

Surprisingly, the elderly lady was the first up. Her stockings were ripped and her knees were bleeding. But she simply brushed them off, adjusted her paper, and continued on her way across the street, dog still in the point position, scanning for further enemy attacks.

The lady with freckles had gotten her red and yellow jogging suit tangled in the chain. Freud helped her get free, then stood with her as she tried to rescue some of her shopping. Freud found himself holding a long and silvery fish. One eye was directed towards him, the other was missing.

"Thank you," the woman said. Her French was a little bit off, like her striped jogging suit and her freckled ringless fingers. He wondered where she must come from.

"It was nothing," Freud finally said. The woman's basket was full again and he couldn't see anywhere to put the fish.

"Are you sure you're all right?" the woman asked Freud.

She seemed to be looking at the area below his waist. Freud saw that his pants were stained with chain oil and garnished with bits of produce and fish scales that clung to them like ornaments on an unwilling Christmas tree. On his shirtfront, once impeccably white, was a big patch that looked like the morning's orange juice, though he couldn't recall spilling it.

"I'm fine," Freud said.

"I live nearby. If you want to get cleaned up. Or borrow something from my husband . . ."

Behind her freckles, her skin was a healthy glowing pink, radiating goodwill and confidence. Freud could imagine her at the beach, broad shoulders, deep chest, long muscular throat, plunging happily into the sea. It was amazing how some people resembled fish, even in their old age. Not himself, of course, with his beard, the grizzled hair that carpeted his chest and belly. Fish and hair. There was an unusual combination. He held the fish out to the woman. She accepted it and then, as though it were a baguette, stuck it head first into a bag overflowing with watercress and radishes. Freud tried to imagine Clarissa or Eleanour returning from the market with a bag filled with a silver fish, watercress, and radishes. Making sumptuous dinners that would send him up and down the evolutionary ladder. Impossible.

"I'll just go back to my office," Freud said. "It's only around the corner."

She insisted on accompanying him. Her name was Yolande. She had been raised in Alsace but had spent the last 30 years in Paris. Freud stopped from time to time, to lean against her handlebars. When they got to the bank they shook hands. Then he turned to open the mesh-reinforced glass door through which he could see the stairs to his office, waiting for him. Part way up he turned. Yolande was watching. When he got to his office he unlocked the door, then went to the front window. The woman was still unmoving on the street, but her face was now turned up towards his. Freud realized that like Napoleon he had slid one hand under his coat. How perfect it would be, as a parting gesture, if he could just withdraw his hand, wave away the window, and send a bird of paradise down to this new last love.

She was smiling at him.

Freud smiled back. Something in her face made it clear she was nobody's sister. She had a wide smile, small gaps between her teeth. He had the impression she realized how foolish he looked, his sallow bearded face hovering impotently above the Banque Nationale de Paris, yet her smile seemed to be saying that he wasn't to worry about it, she'd seen worse. His own smile grew. He could feel the child inside his face, stretching his lips. He didn't want to change the history of the world. Just a few freckles, the odd fish, the knowledge his companion could bear to look at him occasionally with her eyes wide open.

The little alarm on his watch told him he was now due at the lawyer's office. He should telephone his apologies, change his shirt, catch a taxi. He turned away, took a few steps. And then he decided that he would go back to the window. If the woman, if *Yolande*, was still there he would rush down and explain his entire situation to her. He was standing beside his desk. He picked up the package of Marlboro cigarettes. The Marlboro man, firmly ensconced in his eternal white nowhere, was regarding him sternly. Or was there a hint of amusement in his eyes? Freud took out a cigarette. "Mind if I join you?" he asked, and then giggled. Ready to return to the window and meet his fate, he picked up two of the notebooks. He would hide nothing from her.

7 Trevanien paused at the door to Doctor Freud's office. The inside breast pocket of his jacket contained a small packet of cocaine. In Trevanien's opinion, it was strange to think of the doctor using drugs. Yet he hadn't been able to refuse his requests. Curiosity? Pride in being the connection of the nephew of the immortal Sigmund? Habit, most likely. The Doctor appeared not to understand the force of habit. Perhaps the cocaine would help.

There was no answer when he knocked. Trevanien turned the door handle and found it was unlocked. He passed through the small hall, with bathroom and kitchenette on either side, and pushed open the inner door.

At first the room appeared empty. Trevanien looked at the telephone on the doctor's desk. If he called Helen now, he could arrange to meet her for dinner. These days seeing her was becoming essential. That made Trevanien hesitate. As he moved towards the telephone, not entirely committed to this evening with Helen, he decided to start dialling her number just to see if he finished.

Then he saw Freud. The doctor was lying face down on the floor, one hand held to his cheek, the other clutching an unlit cigarette. Beside him were two notebooks, the kind with lined paper and black hard covers that were so common in Parisian stationery stores.

Without thinking Trevanien picked up the notebooks, grabbed the package of Marlboros on the doctor's desk, then left the office. Carrying the notebooks inside his overcoat he went down the stairs, came out beside the bank, crossed the street and turned the corner, went into the Métro.

Six stops later he got out and walked into a café. There he ordered a double espresso and a brandy. He lit a cigarette. It was stale, which meant it was probably from the same package he had left on the doctor's desk several days before. This detail reminded him that eventually the police would want to question him. Of course the fact that he knew Freud was public knowledge. He had even written the interview in which Freud had refused to condemn his uncle's use of cocaine. Results of the autopsy would undoubtedly place this whitewash in a new light. And so the investigation would reach inevitable conclusions. Fortunately, the death of a foreigner was a tragedy of limited proportions.

Trevanien squared the notebooks on the table in front of him. But even before he began reading he knew what would happen. In a few minutes or an hour he would leave the café. The sun would shine on his face, waves of street noise would fold protectively about him. He would amble down the sidewalk, not knowing where he was going. Eventually he would drop the notebooks in a wastebasket. Or leave them on a table. Or sell them. Or forget them. Sooner or later — in a few minutes, an hour, a day, a year — someone would pick them up and read them. After all, nothing could be better than being brought back to life in the eyes of a passing stranger.

8 Freud, breath suspended deep in his belly, listened to Trevanien's footsteps as they receded down the stairs. Trevanien lacked balance. Inner balance. The ability to find the necessary mid-point between fraud and truth. Consequently he had missed both. What Trevanien needed was to forget about his sisters and remember himself, remember the precise focal point of that smooth tawny-haired American dream he'd wrapped around his inner self like make-up caked onto the face of a motherless girl. When Trevanien returned, Freud decided, he could learn inner balance by spending half of each session standing on his head. While Trevanien was upside down, Freud would walk circles around him, reading aloud from his immortal uncle's work. Pacing excitedly, Freud went to the bookshelf, reached again for his favorite volume, *Moses and Monotheism*. He pulled out one of the pages that had become unglued when he threw the book across the room.

It might have been expected that one of the many authors who recognized Moses to be an Egyptian name would have drawn the conclusion or at least considered the possibility that the bearer of an Egyptian name was himself an Egyptian.

Yes, the immortal uncle had been clever. Under that wheezy old man's smile his mind had been all there.

Freud put the book down, secured the locks on his office door, went into the bathroom and took his nail scissors from his shelf. Looking in the mirror he could see that his beard, as unbalanced as poor Trevanien, had begun to go ragged on the right side. Perhaps Trevanien should have gone to bed with his sisters. Suspended between them he might have learned something. In the end, without trimming, what would his beard amount to? A piece of cloth, twisted back and torn along one side. To cover one defect, his scars, he had grown another.

The day his sister shot him in their uncle's study the manuscript of the Moses book had been lying open on the desk. Freud remembered leaning over it, trying to read it. But though he could recall everything from the exact look of his small square fingernails to the burnished light reflecting from the dark wood of his uncle's bookshelves, the words themselves escaped.

His fingers moved involuntarily to his cheek. Left hand, left cheek. Two semi-parallel scars, like the hoofprint of a deer, just below his cheekbone. Between them a peninsula of skin mysteriously intact.

He was clipping his beard, starting as always with the ragged edge, then moving to the other side to match what he'd done, trying to get a preliminary sketch before he actually measured for the final cuts. His telephone rang and his message came on. Between the French and the German he switched back to the ragged side, or what had been, to even up with a mistake he'd made on the scar side. After the tone, Clarissa's voice: "Just calling to know how your work is going." A pause. She had never left a message on the machine before. He would have thought her too dignified to accept an electromagnetic ear. Maybe patients should begin taping their dreams and mailing them in. That way he could throw them directly into the wastebasket without pretending to listen attentively. "Maybe I was too strict." Another pause. Dead air Freud filled by turning on the tap. As he bent his face to the roaring water he could hear the voice beginning again. By the time he straightened up there was silence. He looked at himself. Somehow an island of non-scar cheek had been exposed. He picked up the nail scissors, began working quickly. Soon the beard had given way to a patchy landscape of skin and bristle. He washed his face again, took out his razor blade and shaving cream.

At midnight a pale-skinned man with a scarred triangular face slipped unnoticed from the apartment above the Banque Nationale de Paris and walked along Boulevard Raspail towards the Seine. He was carrying a briefcase and looked, all in all, like the manager of a vending machine business. In his case he carried the passport of such a person.

Given this managerial background along with its necessary propensity for figures, it was no wonder he was able to win a certain amount of money at the Monte Carlo casinos. "The parson," Americans called him, watching the ascetic and devoted way he worked during his week there. After which, as one of those Americans he befriended in Monte Carlo later attested to George Trevanien, he retired to a small condominium in the Swiss Alps where he seemed glad to receive visitors and to live out the remainder of his gray existence surrounded by excellent scenery, a strange collection of books he claimed he was using to research the life of Moses, and two sisters, apparently twins, though one spoke English while the other refused.